The Life of St Michael Garicoits

by

Dominic Inammorati s.c.j.

Published in the United Kingdom by
Society of Priests & Brothers of the Sacred Heart (Betharram)
St. Joseph's Church, Leigh, Lancs.

The Life of St. Michael Garicoits
1st Edition
ISBN 0 9531230 0 6
© 1997 Society of Priests & Brothers of the Sacred Heart
(Betharram)

Designed and printed in the United Kingdom by
Gemini Print Ltd
Redgate Road, South Lancashire Industrial Estate,
Wigan WN4 8DT

Cover Art © E. Emery.

Table of Contents

Acknowledgements

I would like to thank all those who have made this work what it is: in the first place, my Community in Leigh for their support, particularly the Superior, Austin Hughes S.C.J. Further afield, I wish to thank Terry Sheridan in Olton, West Midlands, for his helpful comments. I am greatly indebted to Mary Roach for her most devoted and tireless assistance in proof-reading, and for her invaluable help over translations. My thanks go to the Community at Betharram, especially Jacky Moura, the French Provincial, Pierre Leborgne, Rene Descomps, and Jean Vacque who assisted me in different aspects of research. A big thank you to Liz Emery of Worcester who designed the cover and gave much appreciated advice over presentation.

Original photo of St. Michael.

The Life of St Michael Garicoits

Preface

I n every age, God raises men and women to bring His light to the world in a special way. Michael Garicoits was recognised in 1947 when he was canonised a saint as an example of holiness to the whole Church.

In the changing patterns of today's world, many people are asking questions about life and seeking answers as to where this change is leading; questions ranging from the reason for life itself, and for what is its purpose. Others wonder where God is in all this. Those who believe may ask what does God want me to be, or what does He want me to do? The Church is sent by Christ to teach all nations and has inherited His teaching. Throughout its existence it has developed a tradition of guidance based on God's word which has been applied by saintly and wise men and women inspired by God's Spirit to speak to their generation and pass on this inheritance to the present world. Among these is St Michael Garicoits (1797-1863).

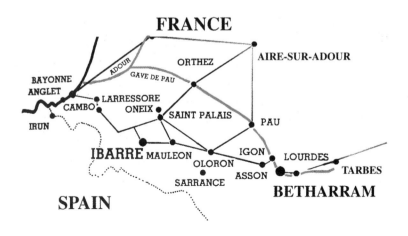

1. Early Years.
Certainly not a Saint.

Michael Garicoits was a French Basque born on the farm of Arnaud and Gratianne Garicoits, in the small hamlet of Ibarre. He was the first of six children, the others being Joanne, Manec, Paulle, and the twins Bernard and Marie; Bernard lived for only four months. He belonged to a hardy and independent race whose origins and language have no apparent connection with any other on earth. Its Echeverrys, Iholdys, Anchiburus, Bussanaritz and Ibarnygaragays are as outlandish to the French as they are to us.

Michael was born in the aftermath of the French Revolution of 1789, when the National Assembly in Paris confiscated all churches and everything the Church in France possessed. Religious Orders were suppressed and all their schools and hospitals confiscated. All clergy had to take an oath of allegiance to the State and cut themselves off from the Pope; thousands refused and chose exile or life without a church building. Bishops were appointed by the State without reference to the Pope; seminaries were confiscated to bring seminarists and professors under State control. This never happened, as too few priests came forward to teach for the new regime. The calendar was changed so that any Christian references were to be wiped out. The only deity that was proclaimed was the goddess of Reason. This was the first time a State had proclaimed Atheism and was going to be the model for Atheistic Communism of the 20th century. Over four hundred bishops and priests and many more Catholic laity were guillotined. Thousands of priests and Religious fled abroad. Many came to England and established schools and hospitals that still stand today.

These atheistic measures were opposed, especially in the countryside throughout most of France. Where loyal Bishops and clergy were driven out, those who replaced them were not accepted by the population and in some cases violently opposed.the Basques, being strongly Catholic, were no exception.

Arnaud Garicoits and Gratianne Etcheberry were married in the registry office in 1796 and then walked over the mountains to Spain to have their marriage blessed in church. As in England and Ireland in the 16th and 17th centuries and till Perestroika in Communist Europe, priests had to hide. Here, they often had to move from farm to farm in order to minister to the Basque faithful, who clung tenaciously to their faith. Michael's grandmother sheltered and hid priests from their pursuers. When the situation was too difficult, they were guided through unfrequented mountain tracks into Spain.

The farm where Michael was born was a traditional structure: a low-lying white plastered building now with a sloping red tiled roof which would have been thatched in his day. As you entered the ground floor, you found a spacious hall with small rooms leading off on either side; the kitchen, and three little living, working and sleeping rooms. Behind these were the stables. In winter, when the weather was harshly cold and the ground deep in snow, animals would be brought in to shelter. On special occasions and family celebrations, everyone would gather in this hall at a large table for a feast or a meal, as they still do today. Upstairs in the attic, extending the whole length of the building, was the grain and the hay loft which opened onto the hillside. This farm called Garaicotchea, meaning 'House on the heights' was set in the beautiful hills and mountains of the Pyrenees.

Life was hard: parents and children worked the fields, digging, planting, weeding, harvesting, and tending the animals, to gain a subsistence from the soil to feed themselves, buy seed, pay for tools and clothing and pay their taxes.

Michael was born in 1797 and was baptised six months later, probably in his farm or the neighbouring one by a non-juror priest who was passing through the area. At this time, France was preoccupied with the Revolutionary war against England and most of Europe. After the great Catholic uprising in the Vendee from 1793 to 1799 was brutally put down by Napoleon, he then turned his ambitions to conquering and enforcing the aims of the Revolution on all Europe; this resulted in the Revolutionary and Napoleonic wars from 1793 to 1815, ending with Napoleon's defeat at Waterloo and banishment to St Helena. Over this period, the force of the revolution to destroy the Church gradually weakened. In addition to this, the Basque country opposed the persecution of the Church for national as well as religious reasons, being to some extent anti-French and favouring the Allied armies advancing under Wellington into France from Northern Spain.

Michael grew up in a Catholic home and learnt his faith and his prayers from his mother. He was no different from any other child. He was well-built and particularly strong, a quality much admired by this hardy mountainous race, who gloried in trials of strength such as lifting and throwing boulders, and speed trials in log-cutting with the axe. He recalled how he would fearlessly swing from branch to branch high in the trees or lie in wait to club down eagles as they swooped on lambs. In later years, in conferences, he sometimes used such anecdotes from his childhood to make a point. Although strong and fearless, he grew in sensitivity . He recounts how he wrenched an apple from his younger brother who was unable to defend himself and who bitterly said to him: 'How would you like it, if someone did that to you?' This made him think and he flung the apple back at his brother. One day, while his mother was not looking, he secretly took some hair-pins from a gypsy . On another occasion, when he was asked by his mother to collect some wood for the fire, he stole some from a neighbour's shed. Without his mother's moral guidance, he said, he would have turned into a really bad character. After these escapades, his mother gave him a stern reprimand and sent him to apologise and restore what he had taken. At night, beside the blazing hearth, he would sit beside her. He recalled how she on one occasion pointed to the flames and impressed upon him that God punishes evil by sending sinners to the fires of hell. Strong stuff! No doubt this salutary fear remained with him, and, as the saying goes, led him into the paths of wisdom. During the winter evenings, his mother taught him by word of mouth his catechism. His road to God began as it nearly always does from the good example of his parents, his neighbours and relations. 'After God, I owe her everything,' he once said.

Michael went to the village school to learn the three R's, plus the elements of Latin, but French was not taught; everything was learnt through Basque. As in most schools in those days, the stick was used liberally. He had a sense of justice which was particularly upset by the beatings that certain blameless children received from the teacher, Old Arnaud. He organised a protest but at the crucial moment when the teacher appeared, the others fled, leaving him by himself. He faced the teacher, who listened to what he said. Michael showed qualities of leadership, and being strong and good at games, was popular. No doubt he played the local game of pelote, a wall game where you hit a rather hard ball against the wall either with your bare hands or more often with a curved raffia racket attached to the hand, from which one could hurl the ball with greater force. You can see these walls and compounds in most Basque villages today.

2. God of Fear, God of Love.

In 1802, Napoleon attempting to win the support of his own people and to further his ambitions of conquering the rest of Europe, including Russia, signed a Concordat with Pope Pius V11 which allowed freedom of worship and churches to be opened. Fr Bidegaray, a priest and local hero, became Parish Priest. He had remained loyal to the Pope and just escaped being sentenced to the guillotine during the Revolution. He encouraged Michael to attend catechism for First Communion even though he was only eleven, which was quite at variance with the Jansenist practice of delaying till fourteen or fifteen. Michael was ready, but almost on the eve of the great day, his mother intervened:

'Be careful, my boy! Confession is a very serious matter. One bad confession means a sacrilege at your First Communion and at every other one afterwards.'

Hell-fire was crackling again. Michael was stunned and perplexed. Being obedient to his mother and with immense sadness, he put it off. This false puritanism in the Catholic Church did incalculable harm which Michael in later years would try to put right. This belief, which is called Jansenism, originated with a monk called Saint Cyr, who was a Basque. He taught an excessive respect for the Eucharist which inspired a fear of receiving it because of God's punishment against any form of unworthiness. God was a God of awe, a judge and a taskmaster, not a God of mercy and love. Michael would never forget this pain; it would help him draw others to a spirituality of the heart.

As was the custom, he was sent at thirteen to work on a farm in the neighbouring village of Oneix. It has been said that this was to repay this family and to supplement his parents' meagre income, especially as there were now four extra mouths to feed. He became a servant to a respected family called the Anghelus. As he looked after the sheep, he began learning by heart his Basque catechism and was instructed for Communion by Fr Barbaste, the Parish priest of the village of Garris. Many were impressed by his eagerness and knowledge, especially Madame Anghelu, who asked the priest if he could make his First Communion early.

'No child may eat the bread which angels fear to touch. Later on, perhaps,' was his stern response. This attitude, which expected perfection, besides being contrary to the Lord's own teaching, made even future priests and Religious sisters receive Communion no more than once a month at the most, and the faithful a few times a year, if that.

Michael recalls that he prayed and reflected in his sadness, especially when he was alone in the hills tending the sheep. One day, the darkness of fear and perplexity was lifted in a deeply religious experience. Speaking about himself in the third person as he sometimes did and advised others to do: 'This is what happened ... He became filled with a light so intense that he felt that it could have reduced him to cinders, had not God intervened, enabling him to withstand the blinding light.'

A moment of revelation like the one that Moses experienced at the burning bush when he came to understand who God really is.

He discovered that God was not a jealous and inhuman God competing against all other human feelings for complete surrender. This too was the false god that the atheists of the 18th century were endeavouring to destroy, but in their case with such devastating results; they raised up man in place of God which let loose the Reign of Terror, the Revolutionary Wars, and a moral and spiritual void which the Church in that century was called to oppose. Michael saw in this vision not the Jansenist god of fear nor the Revolutionary goddess of Reason but the God of Love. He records that he was so absorbed in this experience, some have called it ecstacy, that he walked into one of those stone walls that divide the fields and thus came back to earth with a bump.

On Trinity Sunday, 9th June, 1811, at fourteen years of age, he received his First Communion with much joy in his heart, and great reverence, in the Church at Garris. His cousin Jean-Baptiste Etcheberry, who later became a parish priest, recorded at the process of canonization how so many were visibly affected to see how reverent and enrapt he was at that Mass, as he said: 'like an angel'.

At the reception in the evening of that day, Michael was awarded the prize for the best student of Catechism. He was presented with a Basque translation of a Summary of Christian Perfection by Alphonsus Rodriguez SJ. Many a Religious prior to the second Vatican Council would have read and taken notes from this author in their Noviciate or Scholasticate. Michael always remembered with deep emotion this day and towards the end of his life he fulfilled a long-desired wish to celebrate Mass in that Parish church at Garris, and afterwards, to the delight of the Anghelu family, paid them a visit. The farm still belongs to the family today.

After this day, he felt that God was calling him to follow in the foot-steps of his heroes who had been ready to sacrifice their lives for the faith and to rebuild the Church broken and persecuted by the Revolution. He had been greatly impressed by the life of Fr Dassance, told by Fr Barbaste to the Communion class. Fr Dassance had been arrested by the gendarmes while carrying the Blessed Sacrament to the sick. They took the sacred hosts from him and trampled them into the ground. With the help of a gaoler, he escaped but was later recaptured. Finally, he was sent to the guillotine and publicly executed in the square at Bayonne. Fr Barbaste concluded: 'We ourselves were not holy enough to bear witness to our faith, neither were we worthy to die like him for our faith.'

Very soon after his First Communion, he returned home to work on the farm. Michael was intent on his dream and one day whispered his secret in his mother's ear: 'I would like to be a priest.' Both parents told him that this was out of the question; they could not afford it. Michael told his grandmother, Catherine Etcheberry, of his dream.

One autumn day in 1811, Arnaud with his wife and Michael were digging the vineyard in front of the house while the grandmother was resting in the shade. A few casual words broke the silence. She asked, 'What about Michael?'

'It's time we decided what to do with him,' admitted Arnaud.

'Why not help your children get on in life? Michael is a capable young-ster and he likes study. Give him a chance,' replied the grandmother.

'And who's going to pay?'

Michael intervened: 'God will provide.'

'Tell me, Michael,' said the grandmother, 'if they allowed you to go away and study, what would you do?'

'I'd be off tomorrow morning,' the young man immediately replied.

The following morning, the grandmother, carrying two chickens in a basket, a gift for the priest, walked the five miles to St Palais to see Fr Borda, the local Dean. They knew each other well; she had hidden him in the times of persecution. The priest agreed to secure Michael a place at the school in St Palais, and accommodation with the Anghelu family, who welcomed him as a friend rather than as a servant.

His cousin Canon Etcheberry recorded that very soon after this arrangement, Michael and his father set off to St Palais, carrying a large sack of maize and a shoulder of salted and smoked ham as contribution to his keep.

Parish Church of St Palais

3. From Shepherd
to Servant and Scholar.

From 1811 to 1814, he was both scholar and servant. Each day he walked five miles to and from school. At first he hardly spoke any French, but by hard work in candle-light each night, he became Monsieur Lacazette's best pupil in French and Latin. In these new surroundings he would experience the divisions and conflicts between children coming from families that supported Napoleon and the Gallican Church of the Revolution (Bonapartistes) and those coming from homes that supported the Church and the King (Monarchists)[1]. Michael would remain faithful to what his mother told him as a child: 'France has separated itself from the Pope; we must always put ourselves on the side of the Pope.' Here he made friends with Everiste Etchecopar, a very devout young person, who had a very deep influence on Michael. His nephew, Auguste Etchecopar, was to become the third General of the Society of the Sacred Heart.

As the English, Portuguese and Spanish armies in 1813 were advancing from Spain towards Bayonne, Napoleon's armies were being driven from Northern Spain across the Pyrenees. The Allied armies under Wellington had entered France with 82,000 troops and were met by General Soult with a force of 80,000 including 16,000 conscripts, who had thrown up three defence works across their advance; the first stretched from St Jean de Luz to St Jean Pied de Port, the second from St Jean de Luz to Cambo and the third from St Pe to Ustaritz. After seven pitched battles, Wellington broke through all the lines, capturing St Jean de Luz, St Jean Pied de Port, Bidart and Anglet, crossing the rivers Nive and Adour to the west of Bayonne, and entering St Pierre, the suburb of Bayonne on the south bank of the Adour.[2] In 1814 Wellington had set up his headquarters at Garris for a short while, a few miles from St Palais, before his armies pushed on towards Orthez, Bordeaux and Toulouse. They controlled the surrounding countryside including St Palais. The Bishop sent all his seminarists from Bayonne to the safety of the ancient monastery of Betharram. The Basque country and the Bearn were subject to severe war taxes and all farms could be commandeered to billet the French Army. General Soult's soldiers requisitioned the Anghelu's farm and as Michael, a well-built young man of seventeen could have been conscripted, he was moved for his own safety to the Dean's presbytery in the town of St Palais.

From the last months of 1813 till April 1814 the War with all its horrors of death, looting and the ravaging of local villages and towns by both armies swept through this region. Peace was not restored till after the capitulation of Bayonne to Wellington's army in April 1814.

It is possible that round about this time, the administrator of the Cathedral, Fr Eyherabide obtained a place for him in the Bishop's residence as a servant so that he could complete his studies at the school of St Leon in Bayonne. This priest had been expelled from his Parish of Ibarre-St Just during the Revolution and knew the Garicoits family well. Michael was older than most pupils and much poorer. But he was very keen to learn; too keen for some when he asked the teachers for extra work. Here he pursued further studies in Latin and French classics. Amidst all the political and spiritual turmoil of the times and the War the Spirit of God was inspiring men with vision and deep faith like Mgr Loison, the Bishop, and his successors, to create centres of spirituality and learning in all areas of Catholic education; beginning with the seminaries. The Church had to rebuild itself and at the same time compete with the Enlightenment. In St Leon, many young people went out and made a mark on the world; their influence lasts to this day. Edward Cestac, 1801-1868, a contemporary of St Michael, founded the Servants of Mary and the Bernadines, and Cardinal Lavigerie, 1825-1892, founded the White Fathers of Africa. Edward Cestac's Congregation reclaimed poor girls from the streets while the Bernadines, a contemplative branch of this Order, supported them in their work by prayer. It was to this last Congregation that St Bernadette sought admission but was refused on the grounds of her poor health. Michael's Society of the Sacred Heart would have close links with both these Congregations, as they still do today.

Cathedral of Bayonne.

4. Formative Influences

D espite being sometimes away from school because of duties in the Bishop's house, Michael's ability and hard work took him to the top of his class. In these new surroundings he grew in faith and knowledge. Sometimes, the Bishop would look over his homework.

Here he mixed with a wide variety of people. His most difficult overseer was the cook.

'More often than not I had to endure her fits of temper, so I scoured the pots and pans for her with a cheerful smile. She was good to me by doing my mending and washing my clothes.'

Michael was a good listener. Speaking on obedience many years later, he recalled those days, saying that even in necessity the 'advantages of obedience have their own rewards. You never forget, if like me, you had to beg to live.' He humbly submitted and even managed to become friends with this very awkward character.

The Bishop's Secretary, Canon Honnert, took a lively interest in Michael, who was once again scholar and servant. He studied assiduously, rarely going out during the week except to take the Secretary's dog for a walk.

Having completed his studies at St Leon, Canon Honnert, who was now a firm friend, arranged for him to go to the minor Seminary in 1816, at Aire sur l'Adour.

Michael arrived at the Seminary with a grant from the Ministry of Worship, the rest of the fees being paid by Canon Honnert. For the first time in his life, he could devote himself entirely to his studies. His curriculum included Philosophy, Latin which required learning the Odes of Horace, and French Literature, which included the Fables of La Fontaine. He enjoyed solving problems in Maths, Algebra and Geometry. Abbe Laurence, later to be universally known as the Bishop of Lourdes, at the time of St Bernadette, was his Maths teacher. His studies in History, although sparse, enabled him to appreciate other cultures and the values of the past. In 1817, he began Philosophy, studying Logic, Metaphysics, Ontology and Ethics.He made a special effort to study the background of atheism and the means of refuting it. After two years' study he obtained a certificate allowing him to take a diploma which would be later needed when he opened the College at Betharram.

At this time, he profited from the counsel and guidance of Fr Pierre Larroze who helped him not only pursue his academic studies but kept him faithful to prayer. 'If it is true that I had any piety at that time, I owe it to the counsel and guidance of this saintly man,' he would acknowledge later. From this seminary the best pupils were sent to St Sulpice in Paris, the most prestigious major seminary in France. Michael was looking forward to going there, but he chose to stay near his benefactor, Canon Honnert, who was now ill and needed someone to care for him, which he did. Edward Cestac went instead.

The Major Seminary at Dax.

On the feast of All Saints, 1817, Michael joined eighty other students of theology. His fees were paid fully by the State at the request of the Bishop. His course in Dogma was based on a Gallican manual and in Moral Theology on a manual tainted with Jansenism. The result of this caused him some regret in later life concerning his over-severe attitudes in the confessional towards penitents. He had to make up after ordination for the poor course in Scripture. Besides this, he learnt plain chant and dabbled in Physics and Chemistry. He delved into Church history, especially the period prior to the Revolution, paying particular attention to those who attacked the Church, such as Voltaire and the Encyclopaedists, so that he would be ready to confront their followers when he became a priest. Witnesses of that time say that they were impressed with his prayerfulness and compared him to St Aloyius Gonzaga.

His holidays were often spent in Bayonne with Canon Honnert. 'He was not in sacred orders, yet his holiness lit up his whole appearance. What struck me then, has never faded from my memory,' wrote Canon Pourtalet. Michael spent four years at Dax studying Theology till 1821, when the Rector of Larressore, Abbe Claverie, asked the Bishop for Michael's help in the Minor Seminary.

At the Minor Seminary

Officially, he was appointed as Prefect of Studies for the Juniors, but in fact he was called upon for anything, both in teaching or as bursar. In his spare time, he studied his theology with the help of Abbe Claverie from whom, as he later said, he gained valuable pastoral experience.

Very soon, he became the favourite teacher both in class and in the playground, taking part in games and in feats of strength, carrying several children on his shoulders at the same time. He earned the children's respect and affection 'because he had the gift of keeping us on the right path'. Here he got to know many future priests of the Diocese.

Bayonne Cathedral

14

5. Spirituality of the Heart
Curate at Cambo

Michael was ordained by Mgr d'Astros on the 20th Dec. 1823, at Bayonne Cathedral, with thirteen others. His first Mass was said in the Minor Seminary at Larressore with all the young seminarists present. After Christmas Day, he went home to Ibarre where he said Mass for his family in the Parish Church. We presume there was some local welcome and celebration.

He was appointed to Cambo to replace the former curate. This village had one thousand three hundred inhabitants and was situated on the banks of the Nive. Between the 20th and the 25th of January, he travelled on horseback to this somewhat isolated village, since there were no roads constructed for vehicles till 1843.

Although this village needed revitalising spiritually, it was staunchly Catholic, and during the Revolution became the refuge for twenty priests loyal to the Pope including two who were martyred on the guillotine, Fr Dassance being one of them. Even some lay folk suffered a similar fate for harbouring them. Here, the Constitutional priest was never accepted. During the Revolutionary War in 1894, the area was punished by Bonaparte's army for the desertion of forty-seven conscripts.

In 1813, this area became the scene of many bloody battles between the English and Spanish Armies under Wellington, and the French under Soult. Over 80,000 French troops were defending the length of the Pyrenees and Cambo was fortified against the advancing Allied Forces. Before retreating, Bonaparte's Army sacked and pillaged part of the town.

In this campaign, France lost 30,000 men. One would imagine that Michael would have seen or heard of the distress from these times during his days at St Palais.

Fr Garicoits arrived here eleven years after these events.

He found that the Parish Priest, Abbe Hardoy, was a very sick man, almost totally paralysed. He sought permission to live in his house so as to care for him, which he did. All pastoral work fell on his broad shoulders; he said all weekday and Sunday Masses, besides catechising the young, helping the poor, administering the Sacraments, especially Reconciliation and the Eucharist, and visiting the sick.

He was soon loved by all who witnessed his selfless attention to their needs, both spiritual and material. Just as he was fearless as a child, so through his faith in God's Spirit of love he showed this same characteristic in this parish. A number of anecdotes are recorded. Some parishioners came to tell him that a girl was being dragged down a steep hillside by a runaway horse. He immediately jumped on his, rode down the precipitous slope, to everyone's amazement, and rescued her.

Another occasion was when someone came to him very upset because a member of her family had agreed to fight a duel. He met the two combatants and gently persuaded them to take the Christian way of reconciliation rather than the pagan code of honour.

During a children's catechism lesson in Church, he was told that a builder had fallen from scaffolding and was thought to be in danger of death. In cassock and cotta and followed by a crowd of children, he hastened to the scene to give him the Sacrament of the Sick.

He was made aware by certain parishioners of the anti-Christian influence of certain free-thinkers over people in the town, the mayor being one of them. Fr Garicoits made a point of visiting him. Although this man appeared to treat him with respect, it was not sincere. Fr Garicoits tackled him over his opinions, which were influenced by the anti-Catholic writing of Voltaire, a brilliant writer of biting satire, not only against the corrupt practices of the Catholic Church before the Revolution but against Christianity as a whole. Through his knowledge of these writers and his knowledge of contemporary history and, of course, his deep faith and love of God, he won round this important man and his family. In fact his two daughters were guided by him to the religious life as Daughters of the Cross.

While he was at Cambo, some young people wanted to start a Confraternity of the Sacred Heart. The Parish Priest was not favourable, so they approached Fr Garicoits. He listened and acted. Here was fertile ground for this request. He was aware that this devotion, very popular in

Mosaic of the Sacred Heart,
Church of the Sacred Heart, Droitwich, England.

Spain, was being spread by priests returning from there after the Concordat in 1802. While he was a servant in the Bishop's House, Mgr Loison and Canon Honnert approved the office of the Sacred Heart for the Diocese of Bayonne and Mgr d' Astros, his successor, dedicated his priests to the Sacred Heart, and especially those who became Missioners for the Diocese. Michael was in contact in both Seminaries with priests who had devotion to the Sacred Heart.

He asked Miss Dagorret and friends to see how many wished to be enrolled in the Confraternity. They received over a hundred names. He consulted his friend, Fr Jauretche, who was equally keen. They decided not to register with Paris, but to start the Confraternity in Cambo and call it the Congregation of the Sacred Heart of Jesus and Mary.

It opened with a Solemn Triduum on the 3rd Feb. 1825, with the approval of the Bishop.

The very word 'Confraternity' struck a chord in the hearts of the idealistic young people of the Church of that era; they wanted to convert the pagan ideals of the Revolution, of 'Fraternity' or 'Brotherhood', into a brotherhood and sisterhood in Christ. His Sacred Heart would unite them and bring true 'Liberty' and truly set people free. This was Michael's ideal, too.

There were three main objectives in belonging to this Confraternity which Fr Garicoits was to establish:

1. to win all hearts to love Jesus Christ.

2. to help their neighbours in material needs.

3. to help the Church by seeking vocations and worthy ministers.

The Triduum was a great success, ending with the inauguration of the Congregation of the Sacred Heart on the Feast of the Sacred Heart, which happened to be a Sunday. It concluded with a solemn Benediction. The sanctuary had been decorated with flowers and candles as for a major feast and the whole parish was solemnly dedicated to the Sacred Heart.

Cambo enrolled four hundred members. Surrounding parishes began these Confraternities. Within ten years, over forty Basque parishes had them. In 1826, Fr Garicoits returned from Betharram to establish one at St Just, his home parish. He enrolled eighty-nine members, including his mother and father and brother Paulle.

After he had left Cambo, a five hundred page handbook entitled **The Sacred Heart's Loving Appeal to Faithful Christians** was published. It traced the origins of the devotion through the Apparitions and promises to St Margaret Mary, and was followed by prayers and rules. It was written in Basque by himself and Fr Jauretche. Some of his letters give us an insight into how he felt, and let us share what he said, about the Sacred Heart. He rarely used the term 'Sacred Heart', but nearly always spoke of 'God's love'.

Through the Confraternity, he became God's minister in enabling souls to achieve the ideals that the Holy Spirit had placed in their hearts to become Apostles, to help the poor, to encourage souls to enter the religious life or the priesthood. Here is an extract written to a member of the Confraternity, probably in the Basque country:

To reward you for this generous sacrifice, He gave you His Divine Heart and assured you of the eternal possession of It by the consecration that you have made Him of yourself. With what joy you must have renewed this same consecration the day before yesterday. How many graces will the Divine Heart give you because of the promise you have made. (Letter 2)

In face of difficulties or conflict, he helped souls to persevere without becoming agitated or aggressive, because he encouraged them to trust in the power of God through the Sacred Heart.

Remain in peace in the situation where He has put you, and be sure that when He wishes you to change, He will let you know in a way that will not leave you in doubt. While waiting, do whatever good He sends your way. Do things calmly, gently and without fuss. He wants you to know His peace: that peace which He gave the night before He died. It is to strengthen it and ensure your happiness that He comes nearly every day to establish His throne in your heart ..... Goodbye, my dear Sister, I will not cease to present you through the hands of Mary to the Heart of her Divine Son. Although the graces you need so much come from his adorable Heart, they flow through the hands of Mary to you. He is the source and Mary is the Guardian of the graces that you need so much.' (Letter3)

He often gave prayers to enable people to focus on Jesus and take away negative fears and frames of mind or feelings . Here is a prayer. *'Yes, my Jesus.' Say it in times of trial. This 'Yes' which rests in the heart of Jesus and which He says with so much love to His Father: 'Yes, My Father!' should rest in your heart and come often to your lips in addressing Jesus.*

Here is a sure way to peace. (Letter 6)

An attitude as common then as it is today, is to frighten people into good behaviour, especially children. Here is some advice that he wrote to a teacher:

You ask me how to make yourself feared and loved. Let us say rather how to be loved and respected. Yes, respectful love and respectful affection ..... Respectful affection is maintaining a balance between the false and often destructive worldly love and the cruel charity of the Jansenists, both infinitely removed from respectful affection, which is a precious quality, equally valued by those with faith and those without it.

In an age only too well aware of the results of the permissive society: child-abuse, breakdown in moral standards, broken marriages, stress and mental disorders, and on the other hand, rigid measures based on justice untempered by charity, and rewards just based on material worth or physical fitness, driving people to desperation, St Michael was aware how such attitudes court anger, distrust and hatred; he taught values based on God's love and Christ's parables of mercy.

Picture in
St. Michael's room
at Betharram.

20

6. First encounters with the Religious Life

He met St Elizabeth Bichier des Ages, foundress of the Daughters of the Cross, in the Bishop's house at Bayonne as she was preparing to establish a house at Igon which would be the first in the Bearn and Basque country. He admitted that at this time he knew nothing about the religious life.

Soon after this, two young people approached him, Jeanne Dagorret and Anne Fagalde, the Mayor's daughter, and were urging him to allow them to dedicate their lives to God in the same way as the Daughters of the Cross. If they had not already met these Sisters, they would have heard of their work among the poor and their happiness in living together for God. Michael went to see the nearest convents which were the Daughters of the Cross at Igon and the Dominicans who were at Nay. As he says: 'I was ignorant and worldly and had not the faintest idea of religious life.' Sr Marthe recalls his visit: 'Our poverty amazed him. Although he was not dressed in expensive clothes, he did not give the impression of wanting for anything. He was surprised that we could be so happy when we were in need.'

He then visited the Dominicans and found the convent and the manner of the Sisters much more to his liking.

When he returned, the two girls came to see him and asked: 'Where shall we go?'

His opinion of the Daughters of the Cross was not flattering as he said that they were not well-educated and spoke French badly. He advised them to go to the Dominicans, who were ladies.

In spite of this advice, both of these young persons asked to become

Daughters of the Cross. Jeanne Dagorret was professed as Sr. Timothee; she later went to Ustaritz and became Mistress of Novices in 1829 at Lapuye and died two years later in 1831. Anne Fagalde, the mayor's daughter, became Sr. St. Ignatius. She died in 1831. Her sister, who also joined the Order as Sr Romuald, recorded at the process of canonization: 'Fr. Garicoits found and nurtured nine religious vocations during the twenty-one months he was at Cambo.'

Michael's former rector said of him: 'There are some who attract others by their holiness and whose virtue wherever it is, leaves behind a luminous furrow of light.' He was such a man.

St Elizabeth Bichier des Ages

7. Order. Study. Prayer.

M gr. d'Astros was concerned over the poor state of his Seminary at Betharram. The Rector, Canon Procupe Lasalle, now seventy-five, was losing control of discipline. Not wishing to replace him, the Bishop decided to move Fr Garicoits from Cambo and appoint him as professor of Philosophy, but unofficially to be in charge of reform. Two older priests were also appointed to teach moral and dogmatic theology. At the age of 30 Michael faced a delicate and difficult consignment, as the Rector had been a confessor of the faith during the Revolution and had used much of his money to restore part of the Ancient Sanctuary of Our Lady of Betharram, which had been vandalised and looted after the Revolution. These two new priests were to help Michael restore discipline, renew the spiritual life of the seminarists, and create a better environment for studies. Michael had to face a whole range of problems. Many students were totally unsuitable; the presence of an unsavoury tavern literally on the doorstep did not help matters; regulations were not only lax but unobserved; students could use the general kitchen for cooking their own meals, a servant sold them wine at a fair profit to himself. Spiritually, Jansenism prevailed; Communion was only received once a month at most, the Sacrament of Reconciliation was given with rigorous penances and little charity to the few who went. The programme of studies was not organised.

Michael reported to the Bishop, who told him to go ahead and have patience. All the students recognised that he was a man of God. Many record how they looked up to his example. Soon, over half adopted him as their confessor and spiritual director. They realised that he was not a rigorist but showed understanding and was able to listen, yet he was not afraid to challenge them to seek the highest perfection of the Gospels. Being young, handsome, agile and strong as well as an extremely able teacher, he became very popular and a role model for many who considered him a saint.

He read widely, researched and prepared his classes carefully. Students admired his clear mind and incisive grasp of questions and problems and the presentation and exposition of his subject.

Spiritually, he believed that as future shepherds, the seminarists should be able to lead and should be schooled in prayer. He led the meditations and, as Auguste Etchecopar recalls, on one occasion he spent two hours with them. He was familiar with all the spiritual writers of his era: Bossuet, Olier, Vincent de Paul, Suarez etc., and of course, the Fathers of the Church. The atmosphere and tenor of life in the seminary was gradually transformed. He encouraged the seminarists to receive Communion once a week, some three times a week, which was at first viewed with disapproval and even scandal. The other priests left to Michael all matters of discipline that might cause them any pain. One priest who was then a seminarist recorded that Michael one day took him aside and without any preamble said: 'My friend, what do you mean by this behaviour? Is this the way to become a good priest? Be careful; all this can have serious consequences. You must immediately and completely change this behaviour or I shall not be able to speak for you.' The young priest understood.

'What really struck me was the tone of voice with which he corrected me.' He could feel the force of love in his advice and timely words.

For this reason, Fr Garicoits was greatly respected and loved. Unsuitable characters were gently persuaded to leave. At first, the numbers fell from one hundred and twenty to forty-nine, but in 1830, they had risen to one hundred and forty, the greatest up to that time.

Fr Lassalle died in 1831 and Fr Garicoits was appointed rector at the age of thirty-four. He was also bursar and professor of Scripture and Philosophy. However, Mgr d'Astros had plans to bring all seminarists to Bayonne where a new seminary was being built. That year, the philosophers were recalled and only sixty students remained. In 1833, he ordained the remaining deacons. In 1833 he was in this huge building by himself. Writing to a Church student he says: *You will have ascertained that I am not without titles; from 'guardian of the ex-seminary of Betharram' to even stranger ones. Someone wrote 'Hermit', another 'Chaplain', another*

'Assistant Priest', another 'Resident Priest', the Bishop writes 'Superior of the Seminary'. It would be more exact to put 'Superior of four walls of a vast building'. (Letter 10)

Anticipating the return of the seminary, Mgr d' Astros intended establishing a group of missionaries at the Shrine of Our Lady of Betharram. This idea proved to be a providential step towards the founding of the Society of the Sacred Heart.

The Sanctuary of Our Lady of Betharram and Monastery which became the Seminary for the Diocese of Bayonne (1813-1833)

8. Pilgrims and the Calvary and Shrine of Our Lady of Betharram

B eside the river Gave on the road from Lourdes to Pau is the beautiful Chapel and Monastery of Our Lady of Betharram, a place of pilgrimage since the early Middle Ages. Even before Betharram existed, pilgrims crossed the river here on their way to the shrine of St James at Compostella. As you approach the monastery and Chapel you see the wooded hill on which the ancient Way of the Cross stood. After 1831, Fr Garicoits was responsible for this holy place and this centre of pilgrimage. The first chapel was made after shepherds found a statue of Mary on that hillside. The medieval legend tells that they took it to the parish church across the river at Montaut but in the morning it had returned to the same spot on the opposite bank. This was thought to be a sign that Mary wanted a shrine to be built, which was duly accomplished.

The name, 'Betharram', takes its origin from when a girl fell into the river and was being swept away. As she desperately called on the Mother of God to save her, a lady dressed in white with a child beside her stood on the bank and held out a branch to which she clung and reached safety. In gratitude she later had a branch made in gold which hung over the altar of that first chapel. The place became known as Beth-arram which in the Bearnese patois means 'Beautiful Branch'. So Mary's title in this area was known as 'Our Lady of the Beautiful Branch'.

Throughout the Middle Ages, the Chapel became a holy place of prayer and healing and was increasingly frequented by all kinds of people, including kings and queens, and especially by pilgrims who brought their sick.

The Revolution closed and confiscated this great shrine, but after the Concordat in 1802, the Diocese regained possession of the monastery and Chapel, and pilgrimages began to return in ever greater numbers.

The damage done from the Revolution was quite evident when St. Michael arrived. The organ had been wrecked, the vestments and furnishings and articles of value had been sold. Due to local opposition against further destruction, the building was sold and thus preserved. The first Rector of the seminary after the Revolution, Fr Procupe Lassalle, paid from his own means for the restoration of the roof.

The liturgies were restored and the Shrine was served by the seminary who celebrated once again the major feasts in the Chapel of Notre Dame. The Calvary and Stations of the Cross, even older than the Chapel, had been mostly destroyed or vandalised after the Revolution. Although pilgrims devoutly made the Way of the Cross, the statues were often reconstructed from the broken parts of others with often hideous effect on those who had any sense of art. In the course of years, Fr Garicoits would set in motion a serious and orderly programme of restoration which would be largely achieved in his time.

9. Vision of the Church

B eing responsible for the formation of future priests and involved in lay renewal through the Confraternities, Fr Garicoits was aware from 1828 of Mgr d'Astros' idea of forming a group of Diocesan Missioners who would reside in the monastery, to increase devotion to the Shrine of Our Lady, where sinners could find forgiveness, where the Stations of the Cross would be preached, where retreats for lay men and women would take place in an atmosphere of recollection, faith and devotion. From here the priests would serve the Convent at Igon and the Minor Seminary at St Pe. This vision developed and began to take shape in his mind and heart.

The Vision

The Church in France after the restoration of the Monarchy under Louis XVIII in 1814-1824 burst into life. Religious Orders long suppressed were allowed to return. A new spirit was afoot; a spirit ready for martyrdom and a spirit of courage ready to regain what was lost. In collaboration with the clergy were brilliant lay writers like de Maistre writing on the Papacy, Chateaubriand, a romantic poet whose great work was **Genie de Christianisme,** Montelambert, author of the **Monks of the West.** Although they were not always theologically correct, they generated life into this new spirit.. Michael was aware of the Liberal Movement and took from it what was positive. Great preachers like the Dominican, Lacordaire, put reason in its rightful place and subjected it to God. Through these men a Catholic literary revival took place, not however without controversy and conflict. Fr Garicoits was vetted for his orthodoxy in regard to Lammenaism. Lammenais was a very influential preacher who tried to channel some of the Revolutionary ideas into the Catholic Church in France, namely the authority of the 'sovereign people' in preference to the authority of the Pope. This teaching advocated by Rousseau, one of the theorists of the Revolution, was condemned by Rome. Many theologians and priests in positions of authority were examined concerning fidelity to the true teaching of the Church, as was St Michael. He was liberal in following the 'law of Love' based on Christ's Life, but he always insisted on obedience to the supreme authority of the Pope.

A new Concordat in 1821 was signed whereby thirty new dioceses were established and Catholic life was generously supported by the State, as was the case with Michael, whose seminary fees were paid by the State. New religious Orders were being founded. Bishops of newly established dioceses strongly supported by the laity were founding new Orders to replace those lost in the Revolution, which would spread the faith among the poor and the ignorant in their Dioceses; Bishops like Charles de Mazenod of Marseilles who founded the Oblates of Mary and Mgr d'Astros and his successors in Bayonne, who were God's providential instruments in the foundation and growth of the Society of the Sacred Heart.

Michael was not alone in believing that the time was ripe for a dedicated group of priests to fill the great void in the Church and in the Country left after the destruction of the religious orders by the Revolution. He dreamt of a special troop of apostolic workers drawn from the surrounding towns and villages, knowing the language of the people, aware of their hopes and needs, travelling from parish to parish at the request of their pastors to replant the seeds of Christian life, to popularise real values and preach solid virtue which would produce a wholeness that would be the honour and force of a people in prosperity, and in hard times its greatest reserve.

He saw these men as a means of combating the permissive morals of the Revolution whose sole lawgiver was Reason. Even the clergy were infected with this spirit. Although they preached the faith, daily preoccupations made them forget Christ's words: 'Seek first the Kingdom of God...' Michael recalled that he had seen Bishops weep because priests would not accept reform.

When it became known that Betharram would become a centre for Missioners for the diocese, Michael spoke of his vision with many of the priests on the staff of the seminary with great fervour and persuasiveness.

Even in 1830, he had spoken about his dream, and that of the Bishop, to the seminarists. As a seminarist, Fr Chirou recalls a walk he took with Fr Garicoits which proved to be a turning point in his life when he spoke to him: 'I felt something was struck deep within myself which I shall never forget as long as I live. My vocation was irrevocably fixed.'(Mieyaa TI p544)

Among his first supporters were some members from the Hasparran Missioners of the Sacred Heart which had been disbanded in the Revolution of 1830. Simon Guimon, who was then teaching at the seminary, was the first one to join. He was initially opposed to the idea of vows, but eventually became his first firm supporter.

Michael summed up his programme for his Society in these words:

'If only we could group together priests, following the same plan as the Sacred Heart of Jesus, the Eternal Priest, the Father's Missionary; priests who would have complete dedication and obedience, genuine simplicity and kindness. Such a force would be like commandos on standby for any emergency whenever and wherever the need arises, and especially for the most difficult operations unwanted by others.'

10. Chaplain to the Daughters of the Cross

Fr Garicoits would say Mass each day at the Chapel of Our Lady of Betharram, attend to the pilgrims who wanted confession and counselling, then he would set off to say Mass in the late morning for the Sisters at Igon who would be still fasting from all food and water since the day before. 'How good these Sisters are! How they have to put up with my unpunctuality,' he used to say.

It was in 1826 that Sr Elizabeth first received his advice in the confessional and recognised him as an answer to her prayers. She asked the Bishop if he could be the confessor and director of the Sisters and novices. In 1828 he gave his consent; from that time Fr Garicoits was officially chaplain to Igon.

In those days, there were cultural and language problems between the sisters, who were mainly from Central France, and the postulants and novices from the South West; the Bearn, Bigorre and the Basque country. Fr Garicoits was acquainted with their customs and languages; besides, 'He was a rare priest with a wonderful personality, exceptional discernment, and was a perfect example of virtue,' said Sr Elizabeth. His exuberance, intelligence, faith, and spiritual vitality captivated her immediately. On the other hand he had changed his opinion of religious life and began to admire the self-sacrifice and joy of these Sisters working to give a Christian education to poor girls and to care for the sick. Although twenty-four years apart in age and from different social backgrounds, both were kindred spirits in seeking to spread the kingdom and to save souls through God's love. Fr Garicoits respected and sought her advice. He said: 'You are a saint to work such miraculous changes .... It is to this Good Sister that I owe some understanding of the science of the Cross. Yes, I am telling you, it is she who converted me.'(M493)

After he was appointed Rector in 1831, Fr Garicoits tried to give up the chaplaincy to the Sisters. Fr Guimon replaced him but he was out of touch and 'too dry' for the young postulants and novices. As some began to leave, Sr Elizabeth was alarmed and wrote to the Bishop. Fr Garicoits agreed to return even though he could only come once a month, and when he was particularly busy they would have to come to him at Betharram.

After the seminary had closed, his work with the Daughters of the Cross really began; an attraction for the religious life took root in his heart. Michael was passing through a period of uncertainty and darkness, which at the present time for different reasons many religious orders are experiencing in Europe. In the life and works of these Sisters he saw a divine light that he felt drawn to follow. His conversations with Sr Elizabeth made him realise that 'She had the art of founding and developing the works of God in the midst of darkness, uncertainties and obstacles of every kind; the art of founding and developing them out of that very condition ... And when she discovered the will of God, there was nothing that would stop her, so great was the trust that she had in his promises.' Later he would remark to the Sisters that: 'I am only following her advice and what she has done.'

After the seminarists had left Betharram, he devoted more time to the Sisters and novices. Three or four times a week he walked to Igon for Mass, confessions, meditations and conferences; more than a thousand sisters profited from his direction. Sr Sabine, the third General, said of him, 'He formed our novices and supported our professed so that they remained faithful to their life. He promoted among us the love of Jesus Christ and the poor, a spirit of zeal and simplicity, self-sacrifice and detachment from the world that our founders had impressed on us.'

In the confessional he would exhort the Sisters with 'En avant'-'Go forward, you can be a saint.' His advice was clear, brief, to the point..never having lengthy and fearsome interrogations, yet if need be, he would spend an hour with anyone. His first question was: 'Are you happy?' Then he would listen to the tone of that reply and respond accordingly. Such was his rare and noted quality. How many confessors would do this today or would be capable of interpreting the response, and then be able to act on it? This was what drew many to St Michael and made those like St Elizabeth who was close to God, and following her great vision in evangelization of the poor, realise the precious gifts in leadership and guidance he possessed. Here was a holiness that brought souls close to God and, if they responded, allowed God to do wonders through them. This was true in the lives of so many Daughters of the Cross and many others who sought his counsel.

He remained chaplain at Igon for 35 years. Over those years he visited the Mother House at Lapuye in Poitou for the General Assemblies, gave conferences and preached retreats there and in Colomiers near Toulouse, in Ustaritz near Bayonne and in other houses, as well as making canonical visits to Convents in the Midi. By discernment and intuition, and knowledge of the exercises of St Ignatius, he helped the young discover their vocation by a method he devised from his years of counselling experience. Some of his most discerning and affectionate letters were written to various Sisters in positions of responsibility or when they experienced particular difficulties.

The Convent at Igon.

11. Uncertain Times

As the Sisters were attracting more girls to their schools, people were asking if anything could be done for boys.

A conversation recorded by Bourdenne, the original biographer, between Michael and Marie Perpetue, Superior of Igon, the cousin of St Elizabeth, went something like this:

Sister Marie.   A community of men similar to ours is needed at Betharram.

Michael   Quite so.

Sister M   The seminarists have all gone to Bayonne.

Michael   And who will be the founder?

Sister M   You! Fr Garicoits!

Was this another providential sign?

Michael was faced with mounting requests and their attendant needs. How could he form and establish a group of missioners, found Catholic schools and be responsible for the direction of the young postulants and novices at Igon? How should he proceed in responding to these requests? Where did God's will lie for him? These were uncertain times. Two paths seemed to be emerging; either he should join the Jesuits or found a Society. He was increasingly impressed by the unity and community spirit of the Daughters of the Cross, and grew to admire their fruitful work among the laity, especially among the poor. He was not drawn to communities without vows like the Hasparren Missionaries of the Sacred Heart of which his Basque friend, Fr Garat was a member, or to the Adorers of the Sacred Heart to which his cousin Jean-Baptiste Etcheberry belonged. Michael in his thorough way took all the means necessary and used all his gifts to discover God's will for himself. In 1832, the year before all the seminarists were transferred to Bayonne, he decided to go to Toulouse to make a thirty days retreat (DS222) under Fr Leblanc, a Jesuit, in order to see what God wanted him to do. It seems that he returned for shorter retreats during the following years before and after the founding of the congregation.

After serious prayer and reflection he exposed his deliberations to Fr Leblanc. The conclusion in Fr Leblanc's words was, 'God wishes you to be more than a Jesuit; follow your first inspiration, which I believe comes from heaven, and you will become the Father of a family that will be a Sister to ours... I believe that for the time being God wants you to stay at Betharram. You can do good there by ministering to the pilgrims and by giving spiritual support to the little community at Igon.'(M 522)

His path was made even clearer when he visited Mgr d'Astros at Toulouse who said: 'Go and start your work; and without preceding Providence, follow it with generosity and perseverance in all its signs.' He never forgot this inspired advice and used it in helping others to reach decisions. When he returned to Betharram he knelt and prayed before the statue of Mary. 'I have experienced in the depth of my soul a most extraordinary feeling that makes me sure of my project and encourages me to carry it out.' Between 1837 and 1838 he returned again for further direction to Fr Leblanc, who gave him a Summary of the Jesuit Constitutions. From this retreat and the reflection on the Summary came his Manifesto proclaiming the primacy of love in community life. Later, Bishop Lacroix did not agree with Michael's wish to adopt these constitutions since they would take the community outside his jurisdiction and place it under Rome. Michael's holiness and wisdom grew in coping with this conflict which was never resolved in his life-time. Some writers of his life have seen this as an injustice and have emphasised the division between the Bishop and himself. Looking back, we may see this conflict as providential.

12. Difficulties in putting a dream into practice.

L ike many founders St Michael had considerable difficulty in realising his dream, especially when it was a question of persuading those in authority to allow him to found the Society. Many years later in a letter to Didace Barbe in Argentina in 1859 he wrote:

'Monsieur Guimon and I went to see Mgr. d'Arbou (the new Bishop) *in 1832 to ask his permission to form a Society of priests at Betharram. His Lordship accepted us simply as priests of his Diocese. We had to wait like Lazarus in the tomb. We had our triduum of suspense. The Bishop turned to Mgr. Laurence* (The Vicar General) *and said, 'It will cost me at least a thousand francs a year; but someone will have to look after the house at Betharram.' Then the unfortunate thought enters one's mind, especially to those who have no mission to take on, that they do not want us or they do not trust us.'(Letter 188)*

He compared this period of waiting to the time that Lazarus spent in the tomb before the Lord brought him back to life. The suspense was because the Bishop's answer was not formally given till two years later. During that time they persevered but suffered from those with influence and power:

'We have had inevitable opposition and understandable suspicion. In order to win the right to serve the Church, we had to struggle against the Church. Then after so many serious trials, the spiritual authority had to surrender and covered us with its mantle, as it recognised in us the signs of a Divine consecration. As a result we have been accepted in its ranks, but without ever losing the seal of that unfettered impulse which created us. Our power to act comes from this spiritual authority,' meaning the approval of the bishop. But he never lost sight of his trust that *'our life is from God*

and from ourselves. This is a fact.' (Writings of St. M. No. 1159)

Like many founders of yesterday and today, the impulse that Michael felt was the charismatic impulse. The impulse which would not be stopped or confined by those who worked by the rules, by existing canonical structures, because his inspiration was to found a way of religious life that would not be defined by works, place or history, but would be defined by what it is; not by what others thought it would do, but by what Michael knew it should be. *'Our life is from God'.* His response and that of the Community in living by this impulse of the Spirit generated life and the Society became a sign which could not be ignored. In this sense, that life would be also *'from ourselves'* and would be the reason for the Society's existence in the Church then, and in the Church of the future, as long as it remains faithful to that impulse.

The seminarists had all left Betharram. Michael was on his own and had prepared and just celebrated the Holy Year Jubilee at the Shrine of Our Lady. A little school was now opened to give a Catholic education to local children. St Michael had care of minor seminarists and some students, chaplaincy to the novices at Igon, and mounting demands from the shrine and its pilgrims, as well as his ministering to the Parish of Lestelle.These times of waiting were difficult as this letter to a former Church Student indicates:

It is quite a while since I received your kind letter. I felt very touched by this token of your friendship, and you may rest assured that I will always take a lively interest in all that I hear concerning you. If I am behind in replying to you it is not a sign that I have forgotten. You are often in my thoughts. How could I forget a young man that I always have and always shall hold in close regard? All the confusion caused by adapting to a new way of life, and the overwhelming amount of preparations for the jubilee, that we managed to complete the day before yesterday, are the reason for my delay.

You see that I have no title. This new position which one would imagine would afford me a little rest, requires even more activity from me, until people of good will come to share my loneliness, my poverty and my work. Frs Chirou and Carrerot will probably be the first two to come. As regards my former colleagues I have not much to tell you; Fr Sartolou is Parish Priest at Gan; Fr Cambot is chaplain to the Royal College at Pau; Fr Guimon gives retreats in various parishes.

Mgr d'Arbou, the Bishop, was not opposed to the Society, but saw difficulties which made him hesitate before making this decision. He allowed the Society to begin without interference. In 1834 he gave his permission. Despite a lack of clergy for parishes in his diocese, he allowed priests who requested to join the Community. He wrote: 'I am far from putting obstacles in your path, it will be a pleasure to support it.'(Letter M Vigneau 14th June 1836)

Sometimes priests had to wait.

'This year there are very few ordinations to cover the different needs of the diocese,... Next year there will a considerable number of ordinations to cope with these needs. Those of Betharram will not be forgotten.' (Letter to Michael Garicoits, 5th Jan 1836).

Mgr d'Arbou was a friend and spent time at Betharram when he could. However, the diocese was not happy in giving financial support to Betharram. In fact, Michael had to find his own support, and greatly relied on Providence.

Mosaic in the Church of the Sacred Heart, Droitwich, England.

13. First Companions

etween 1833 and 1837 sixteen priests asked the Bishop to join
B Betharram. The choice was made with care; only seven were accepted. In 1835, five came to make up the first community. Three had been
members of the Sacred Heart Missioners of Hasparren: Simon Guimon,
Pierre Fondeville and Pierre Perguilem; the others were Jean Chirou, who
had been taught by Fr Garicoits, and Louis Larrouy, a Parish Priest.

'In October 1835, the Community of Betharram was Frs. Garicoits,
Guimon, Perguilem, Chirou, Larrouy and Fondeville, who wished to give
themselves a rule to sanctify themselves. They adopted the rule of the
Missioners of Hasparren, and without doing any noviciate other than will-
ingness to glorify God, save souls and sanctify people, they unanimously
elected M Garicoits as their Superior, promised him obedience, poverty,
and renewed their vows of chastity and gave him their little purses.'
(Chronique de Notre Dame. Fondeville). Thus they held all in common like
the first Christians recorded by Luke in the Acts of the Apostles.

Missioners of the Sacred Heart

The great means of re-evangelising France in the 19th century and to
some extent Western Europe was by Parish Missions. It was the most powerful instrument of French Catholicism after the Revolution. Missions
instructed the laity, preached Christian morality, attacked the paganism of
the Revolution, often with patriotic and hell-fire sermons intended to
inspire fear and respect for God and the Church. The Minor Revolution in
1830 dissolved Diocesan Missionary Societies like the Hasparren
Missionaries and incited mobs to destroy Crosses erected during Missions
given between the fall of Napoleon and death of King Charles X. These
events sent shock waves through the Church, but after the accession of
Louis-Phillippe and then Napoleon 111, the Church was not hindered, and

in some cases, was even helped in redeveloping its missions. Former Orders like the Jesuits, Vincentians, Capuchins,etc. returned and many new Congregations were founded. During this period many new orders for men and women were founded in France; in 1835 the Priests of the Sacred Heart by Michael Garicoits, in 1836 the Garaison Fathers of Lourdes, the Marists, Sacred Heart Fathers of St Quentin, Sacred Heart Fathers of Issoudon, the Oblates of Mary, etc., and forty-five Diocesan Missionary Societies. A gradual spiritual renewal was taking place all over France for the rest of the century and beyond.

At Betharram, all the priests took part in missions and sometimes they linked up with the Garaison Fathers of Lourdes who were sent by Bishop Laurence of Tarbes and Lourdes to be trained there.They formed two groups. These priests gave missions in parishes, retreats for First Communions, for schools, for seminaries, for religious orders, to pilgrims that came to the Shrine for a retreat.

Fr Garicoits because of his work would be mainly involved in the immediate vicinity. Giving Missions was hard work. Fr George Higuere writes of 'rising at four o'clock in the morning' and spending very long hours in the confessional. The Mission began with Mass in Latin when the Rosary was recited. This was followed by Mission exercises of prayers and blessings and processions. Each day had instructions which followed the Diocesan Programme, usually preached with drama and power; sinners were reconciled, marriages put right, and all entertainment shut down such as dances and cabarets. The day ended with Benediction. Sodalities and Associations were vigorously promoted, particularly the Confraternity of the Sacred Heart so that when the missioners had gone, the good works and prayers of these Associations would continue. At the end of the Mission the Parish would make a dedication and erect a huge cross in a public place. Such was the way in which Michael Garicoits and his Community became instruments of the Spirit.

14. Chaplain to the Sanctuary of Our Lady of Betharram

Before the Revolution, there had been at Betharram a community of priests of the Holy Cross founded in the 17th century by Hubert Charpentier. They organised the liturgies and provided a schola cantorum for the occasions of pilgrimage, especially for the major feasts like the 14th and 15th September, the feasts of the Exaltation of the Cross and Our Lady of Sorrows. During the upheaval of the Revolution, the priests were dispersed and now Fr Garicoits with his Community was to restore this holy place. Fr Fondeville was placed in charge of the pilgrimages and Fr Garicoits took his place in the confessional, where he became God's instrument of conversion and change. Many came from the surrounding towns and villages to Mass and Services. Others came for advice and confession.

One example of St Michael's spiritual influence was in the meeting with Marie Bonnecaze. Known as Maria, she was from Haute-Marne and was spending a holiday at Nay near Betharram at her uncle's. While there, her two cousins took her to Betharram. After looking around the Sanctuary, the cousins went to Confession to St Michael. Marie followed, but while in conversation with St Michael whom she had never seen before, he was called away. He asked her to stay and promised to return in two hours. It is not recorded what transpired in this first meeting, but she waited and stayed in the Chapel in prayer. This time the meeting lasted more than two hours. At the process of canonization, she related, 'Before meeting Fr Garicoits, I was entirely focussed on a worldly way of life and was about to get married; something my family was looking forward to. After this meeting, I was completely changed. I felt no taste for the world that I had known and in spite of the cost, I decided to do the will of God, whatever that was.' Her life changed. She went to daily Mass and Communion, gave up her former leisure-pursuits and vowed herself to works of charity. She

Pilgrims at Betharram.

looked after a lady with cancer whose condition drove most people away; she dressed her wounds and cared for her soul. Before this meeting she only dreamt of marriage; now only of God and the religious life.

She made a decision to make a retreat at Betharram. To avoid alerting her uncle or her family, she, with her cousin, asked her uncle if they could spend two weeks at Arudy, twenty kilometres away. Not suspecting anything, he agreed and got them two horses. They set off, but rode to Igon where they told the Sisters of their scheme. The Superior, Sr St Jerome agreed to contact St Michael. They both disguised themselves as peasants and arrived at Betharram dressed with great head-scarves over their hair. St Michael knew nothing about their plans but when he recognised them, he could not stop laughing. He found them lodgings with the family in the farm opposite the monastery. Without wasting any time, they began their retreat. Their programme was quite rigorous: Mass and Communion, four daily meditations, two examinations of conscience, and a visit to the Blessed Sacrament. He put the exercises of St Ignatius in their hands and prepared each of them briefly each morning, then received them in the confessional twice a day. After a week, Marie-Claude, the cousin, decided to enter the Daughters of the Cross, and Marie Madeleine the Sisters of

43

Charity. The family at first opposed Marie-Madeleine.

From this meeting there followed a correspondence. This is his reply to Marie-Madeleine:

My Dear Sister in Jesus Christ,   24th Nov. 1842.

It is a few days since I received your letter of the 24th Oct. Each day I have thought I would reply but I have always had to give way to more urgent jobs which need my supervision; first a reunion of more than two hundred Sisters gathered at Igon and later, some decisions to be made about the Missions. On top of that, sorting out places for pupils who are coming to us in larger numbers than ever. Today I am taking a break from all other business.

I am acutely aware of your situation and the sorrow that you feel from it. I would like with all my heart to help you overcome the obstacles that prevent your realizing your plans which are, I do not doubt, the designs of God Himself. But I can only pray and ask for prayers to Almighty God so that He will grant you the grace of overcoming your father's opposition and obtaining the consent you want so much. While you wait, try to imitate Mlle Lagelouze from Bayonne who is, at long last, a Daughter of Charity. You know that she only shared this happiness after going through similar trials. You have not forgotten that she submitted to them in the same way as Jesus did. How utterly unshakable she was in her intentions. Yet at the same time she remained gentle, considerate, humble and devoted. For example, she was always the first to take her father's coat. She became more and more loved by God and her father.

Do as she did. Like her, behave pleasingly to God and pleasingly to your father and I venture to hope that in good time you will get the same results as she did. Use the same means to win over both. I do believe this will work for you too. Like her serve both with good grace and ever increasing zeal; above all, refuse nothing that your dear and respected sister asks of you; I should like to hope that you will obtain in the fullness of time what she obtained.

The canticle of the new Adam is, 'Here I am.'

Farewell my good Sister. Remember that patience, courage and perseverance will win the day.

All yours in the Hearts of Jesus and Mary

St Michael did write to her father who did give his permission. She became a Sister of Charity and worked in Egypt and Chile. St Michael had opened up a life that would follow a completely new path, a path of much greater fulfilment, one dedicated to the poor for Christ. From Alexandria she wrote in 1849: O Betharram, how can I forget you.... I can never find words to express the gratitude to Fr Michael Garicoits. I am so filled with happiness to know that he remembers me at the altar.... Assure him of my love and gratitude.... Every day I repeat with so much pleasure the prayer that I have taken from him and which you must know: 'Here I am.' Mieyaa Vol 1 Letter 20

Many came to seek Fr Garicoits's counsel over a great number of matters; bishops, priests, and lay folk in their various capacities.

The only photo we have of St Michael was sent to Count Severin Uruski, of Polish descent, who was working as an official of the Czar of Russia. He tended to stay with his cousin in a chateau not far from Betharram when visiting the Spas in the Pyrenees. While in the area, he frequented the Sanctuary of Our Lady. In doing so, he came to know St Michael, whom he consulted. Before taking up his post as Chamberlain to the Czar, he made a week's retreat under the direction of St Michael. Both became friends.

This extract is from a fragment of a lost letter in which he enclosed the photo taken in August 1861.

P.S. I hope you will not be upset to accept this photo of my old carcase.

Count Uruski records that 'Fr Garicoits is one of the holiest priests I have met.'

Betharram offered shelter to those in distress. In 1835, the Community received persecuted priests and Religious expelled from their houses and monasteries in Spain. The Society offered hospitality to a community of Spanish Capuchins of priests and brothers. While they stayed at Betharram, he discovered and realised the importance of the vocation of brothers and how they not only lived the Religious Life but helped the priests in their ministry. This sowed the seeds in his mind of the future Community of Brothers of the Sacred Heart at Betharram.

Although the Community was, as Michael said, a 'divine consecration' or witness to the evangelical counsels of the Gospel which was recognised by the Bishop and the people, he could not act without the Bishop's consent even in these matters, as this letter to Bishop Lacroix of Bayonne suggests.

I seem to have some recollection of having suggested for the attention of Your Excellency the matter of Don Ignatio de Paleres, Canon, secretary and companion in exile of the Bishop of Barbastro and measures proposed for his joining us at Betharram. I understood that he had changed his mind so I was not expecting to see him in our house when I returned from Bayonne.

However he came while I was away and begged so desperately to be admitted that they felt they could not deny him at least a temporary shelter. We have considered this in council and concluded that we should ask your Excellency to allow us to continue our hospitality to this respected priest who deserves so much for many reasons.

He is a very holy priest. Only his remarkable fidelity kept him beside Mgr Barbastro during his long years of exile. Everyone has a story to tell of the endless good he has done since coming to stay in Pau. It would be no expense to us. As soon as people knew that he had retired to Betharram, goodness knows how many good souls offered to pay his expenses.

I would be grateful, Monsignor, if you would let me know your wishes on this matter. If you agree we will keep this good man here though I would not be able to predict at this moment for just how long. (Letter 37)

'Canon Paleres remained at Betharram and died there in 1847. When St Michael wrote to Bishop Barbastro reinstated in his See, he replied, 'With tears and a sad heart I read your letter on the death of my dear secretary and companion in exile.... Words will not express my gratitude to yourself and your Community for the care you have shown to my dear secretary during his long illness and in the last days of his life. May God reward you.'(Mieyaa)

There is a story told of an English Protestant in those days of English bigotry and prejudice against the Catholic Church. Being curious to know what happened in Catholic Churches, he entered the dimly lit chapel and

watching from behind a pillar, saw a priest genuflect before the altar and then kneel in prayer. He was so impressed by his fervour and prayerfulness that he later approached the priest, who was Fr Garicoits, and asked him for instruction in the Catholic Faith.

Fr Bourdenne recounts that on the special feasts such as the Nativity of Our Lady and the Exaltation of the Cross, great crowds of pilgrims from the surrounding regions came to the magnificent liturgies at this Shrine. Some came on foot in small groups, but the majority in carriages of all colours, shapes and sizes, which created a picturesque sight; all these groups praying or singing their native chants in their own dialects or languages. The programme of devotions began in the evening, on the vigil of the Feast. The chapel was packed for two days. Confessions were heard non-stop and Communions went into the thousands. To be present was a joy so uplifting, not only for the priests but for all the pilgrims. Crowds were praying together with such fervour, and so completely absorbed as they listened in rapt attention to those great preachers; one could feel the swelling emotion as with one voice they consecrated themselves with faith and love to Jesus.

Coat of Arms of Lestelle-Betharram.
Depicting the Calvary and the star from which it takes its name.
The oxen conveying its agricultural community - the motto is in the local Bearnese dialect - "your light ... the star..."

48

Prayer of Consecration

O Mary, Here I am
Accept us and present us
To your Divine Son.

Hail Mary

Jesus, Here I am.
Accept us from the hands of your Holy Mother and
present us To Your Father

Soul of Christ, sanctify me...

God, Our Father, Here I am.
Accept us from the hands of Your Beloved Son.
We surrender ourselves to Your love.
Here I am, O God. without any conditions.
I am entirely Yours now and for ever,
Under the guidance of the Holy Spirit *
(and our Superiors,)
Under the Protection of Jesus and Mary, Our Guardian
Angels and Our Patron Saints.

Our Father.

*For members of the Society

15. Restoration of the Chapel and the Stations of the Cross

A s Chaplain, he was very much in touch with the people of the whole locality and with their profound religious aspirations. In 1836, Fr Garicoits undertook the restoration of the walls and ceilings of the Chapel of Notre Dame and became a builder in the literal sense. Writing to Sister Jerome, Daughter of the Cross, who had been his first postulant from the Bearn, he indicates that his plans did not always meet with his Community's approval. *'They do not want me to replace the wooden altar with a marble one; they say it would be out of place.... Please let me know what you think.'* She was a kindred spirit and her practical advice was sought on more than this occasion. In 1849, he did have a marble altar built on the sanctuary which stands there today and another was built at the same time in the chapel of Compassion which was given by Canon Palleres who had been welcomed into the Community from Spain. In 1845, he commissioned Alexandre Renoir to create the beautiful statue of Our Lady of Betharram which is now seen above the main altar. In 1860, he commissioned the artist Dauvernge to paint the Sanctuary. Unfortunately, this was not realised because of his death.

For a long time there was a desire to restore the ancient Way of the Cross situated on the hill behind the Monastery. Fr Garicoits was introduced to Alexandre Renoir,a young Catholic artist and sculptor. Being well aware of the power of the press and its effective use in rousing interest and financial support even in those days, Fr Garicoits kept up a regular correspondence with the Editor of the **'Memorial des Pyrenees'**. Between 1842 and 1845 a series of articles was published about his work to restore the Calvary. Renoir's novel and extraordinary work had excited much interest and admiration, as well as praise from Fr Garicoits. The local press eagerly took up his letters.

Mary meets Jesus. A. Renoir.

Alexandre Renoir.

'We print the following letter giving you the latest developments reached in the restoration work on the ancient Calvary, the object of so much veneration in our country.'

Then it proceeds with Fr Garicoits's letter:

We must express our gratitude for your unremitting efforts to promote all that is beautiful and worthwhile. Without doubt these works would have stayed hidden from human eyes or remained unfinished, if you had not brought them to the attention of the public.

Work on the Calvary of Betharram is making good progress. The 4th Station of the Cross, the Scourging, is ready. We hope that the work will be well received. The artist's deep knowledge and expertise in the field of classical sculpture will not repeat the unfortunate works of the past. He does much more. The essential idea is to present Our Lord, when at the mercy of His torturers, in a realistic way which not only conveys His human feelings, but sees beyond the physical and into His Spirit. It cannot be said too strongly; without this last proviso it could not be called Catholic Art.

Should one look to find triumphant signs of life where only death is expected? Who would want to see along the Way of the Cross a long line of profane subjects? The proper character of this work should be truly relevant to the spirit, and from this point of view one can admire what value a craftsman of talent using all the resources of his skill has given us.

Now the Calvary is beginning to appear quite transformed; you can already wander around a large area occupied by the new works of Art. All those monstrosities of the past have disappeared.

It is true that the top of the Calvary is empty since we are not sure whether we consider a painting is appropriate for the Stations of the Cross, but it will all come together, if everyone will be part of this venture which began with so much enthusiasm that it should not stop now. Let us hope that following the example of Him whose footsteps he is retracing, the artist will be able to sustain to the end the enormous burden of this work so that he will be able at the end to proclaim with satisfaction: 'It is finished.' Letter 20 Vol 3. written in March 1843.

Our Lady of Betharram by A. Renoir.

Michael Garicoits was not just resident at the Shrine but had become a public figure contributing not only to the spiritual renewal of the locality but also to its cultural values and deeply felt Christian sentiments. Through Fr Garicoits the Congregation had at heart the aspirations of the people, which is a very important aspect in the growth of a Religious Community.

After the Marquis of Angosse, a local family, offered to restore the beautiful Chapel of St Louis X111, which was the 5th Station of the Cross, Michael commissioned Renoir to create this scene in Carrara marble.

The 5th Station, the Crowning with Thorns, he writes in 1843, *has been installed in the Royal Chapel at Betharram. It is here that one of the noble families has shown a desire to venerate their saintly ancestor. There is no call to emphasise the qualities of these sculptures by Renoir which always portray the same perfection and poetry! If there were any observation to make, it is that this Station, by the striking posture and evil character of the figures, is without doubt the most remarkable work that has come from the hands of this artist.*

M Combalot (who had introduced Renoir to Fr Garicoits) *has written to ask to be one of the patrons of this work and has visited us several times. He was able to appreciate and congratulate his artistic friend in having created a great and truly Christian work of art. He has employed him, as one hopes, to continue in this manner, assuring him that it is in the profundity of Catholic thought that he will be able to draw forth a powerful inspiration for those who aspire to make men and women better people.*

Michael Garicoits wrote again to the paper on 17 June, 1845.

You have frequently made your readers aware of the restoration of the Calvary of Betharram. This splendid work begun and continued by M Renoir, with so much talent and dedication, has already progressed a long way. Eight bas-reliefs adorn the first eight chapels. After the Agony in the Garden and Betrayal of Judas which M Mazure spoke of with so much interest comes the Station depicting the Saviour before Caiaphas, then the Scourging which is followed by the fine Chapel of St Louis with the two small and elegant hermitages erected by King Louis X111 and restored by the generosity of the Marquis of Angosse. There one finds the Crowning with Thorns and a little distance away, Jesus Condemned to Death.

Climbing further, one comes to Jesus carrying his Cross, and finally, you come to Jesus being Nailed to the Cross, where our artist has surpassed himself.

Much has been done; it remains for us to complete the three bas-reliefs and the Crucifixion. An unforeseen accident is at present preventing important work. While making soundings on the walls of the Chapel on top of the Calvary we have learnt that they are in a state of collapse. We have consulted experts who have confirmed our fears and we have sadly come to the inevitable conclusion that the Chapel must be completely rebuilt if we can safely install the bas-reliefs that were intended for it. A considerable sum is needed for this construction, added to the sum also needed for the completion of the Stations which will be in the region of twelve to fifteen million francs and we are in no position to realise that sort of amount. From four years of making every sacrifice to pay non-stop huge multiple debts, we are now drawing on our last reserves and in addition we are paying M Renoir a bonus of three thousand francs, without doubt far below adequate remuneration for his talent and our indebtedness to him, but sufficient to make it impossible at this time to continue the work which we are so keen to accomplish and which interests the whole region.

Fortunately we are assured that it will be completed. With the help of the General Council of the Basses-Pyrenees who have offered us a loan, and a guarantee from some generous souls, the new Chapel will rise from where the other stood; and without any danger the set of stations can be safely erected there; this locality will be endowed with a monument unique of its kind.

M Renoir, to whom the region should be for ever grateful, is going to Italy to study the major works of art. There at the tomb of the Apostles he will draw inspiration in keeping with the importance of the subjects that remain to be commissioned.

I believe, M Editor, that you intend to continue your kind support. Please accept our sincere thanks for the active part you have taken in this work, and for the interest you have shown in promoting it publicly. Letter 28

In 1845, in spite of so many other commitments, he was able to organise funds and appeal to local authorities by writing to the Prefect of the

Basses-Pyrenees for the restoration of the Chapel of the Resurrection at the top of the Calvary.

Last year, you very kindly presented our case to the General Council for the restoration of the Calvary at Betharram, and I was duly accorded a grant of one thousand five hundred francs. All well-meaning people of this locality appreciated the fairness and propriety of this gesture. Speaking personally I can only repeat what I have already told you, that I shall always remember with the deepest gratitude your efforts on our behalf.

The time has come, Monsieur, when I need to withdraw money from this account. I await your approval to begin work on the Calvary, which I was obliged to suspend through lack of funds. With the grant of the three hundred francs and other help that I have already received, I am about to put in hand the work of replacing the former chapel, now in a state of collapse, with a new one which is intended to receive the three bas-reliefs that are to be made.

This is now the Chapel of the Resurrection built between 1866 and 1868 by his successor Fr Chirou from the design of Fr Pailloux SJ and decorated by Br Jean-Marie Pujo SCJ. The inspiring statue of the Risen Christ is by Fabisch, the author of the statue of Our Lady of Lourdes in the Grotto, based on St Bernadette's description.

In 1860, Fr Garicoits informed the Bishop that the Emperor Napoleon 111 and the Empress visited the Chapel.

Today, we received a visit by someone from the Chateau at Pau, who came from the Ministry to see where the organ would be placed, which has been given by His Highness the Emperor. We have been told that it will be here in August.

In conveying to you this news, I ask Your Eminence to be good enough to let me know if I am indebted in any way to the Emperor or Empress who have just arrived at Eaux-Bonnes (Letter 521) which was not far from Betharram.

A nice little touch occurs in a letter sent at this time to Fr Barbe in Buenos Aires.

The day before yesterday, I was due to go to Nay.... I was on the bridge when a carriage passed by. I am not sure how I greeted the lady who was inside. She very graciously returned my wave with a friendly and modest smile which struck me and made me suspect it was the Empress. In fact it was. That is how I saw the Empress without expecting it, just after I left your sister....Letter 522

The Emperor Napoleon III and Empress visiting the Refuge for girls at Anglet founded by Fr Cestac. Later, St Michael appointed Canon Etchegaray of the Society as Chaplain to the Sisters and girls at this Residence.

16. Christian Education of the young

In 1837, St Michael opened the School of Notre Dame. In a letter written to Fr Bourdenne, in 1855 then experiencing difficulties in the foundation of the College of St Francis at Mauleon, he recalls his own problems:

How was the school at Betharram founded? I began by telling only Monsignor about the project of starting a school. Elicabide was present although not yet qualified. The Bishop approved the project which was effected a year after his approval with Elicabide and Arabehere working there by themselves. God clearly blessed this enterprise. Soon there were one hundred and fifty to two hundred pupils. Elicabide was practically alone, and really devoted himself to it. God worked wonders in their souls and the school's reputation grew. We had eventually to dismiss Elicabide, which event took place in Oct. 1839. Everyone was against his removal in spite of the things he did, but he refused to accept the conditions we set and so dismissed himself.

The school was then placed under the headship of M Lacazette while we were waiting for Fr Barbe to get his teaching certificate. Then the struggle with the Academy and inspectors from Pau happened. In these problems I was left entirely on my own, without any help, while being obliged to tell no one; it was a time of silence and especially of patience. That is how it all began. Letter 108

There were some introductory problems: he had to overcome opposition from his own Society; the anti-Catholic University in Pau tried to kill his project by forbidding him to teach Latin and take in boarding pupils; after only a year he had to sack the first headmaster, M Elicabide, for soliciting unauthorised money from his pupils.

Writing to his cousin Fr Jean Baptiste Etcheberry, two years later, he

In the Pyrenees

Garacotchea, the farm at Ibarre where St. Michael Garicoits was born and grew up.

The small Parish Church at Ibarre, where St. Michael's family worshipped and where he celebrated Mass.

The farm at Oneix where Michael worked , and later lodged while at school in St. Palais.

The Church at Garris, where Michael made his first Communion.

Cambo-les-Bains, The Parish Church where he was curate.

Cambo-les-Bains.

The interior of the Church where St. Michael helped to found the Sacred Heart Confraternity.

Betharram

The Chapel of Our Lady of Betharram.

The interior of the sanctuary of Our Lady of Betharram.

iii

A view of the Chapel, the Monastery and Stations of the Cross, and the College of Notre Dame.

The Statue of Our Lady of Betharram over the High Altar, by Alexandre Renoir 1845.

A painting of Our Lady of the Beautiful Branch, by Joseph Castaing 1908.

View of the Ancient Bridge of Betharram, the Chapel of St Michael Garicoits and the Chapel of St Louis of France, which is the 5th Station of the Cross, the Crowning with Thorns.

The interior of the Chapel of St Michael Garicoits

Views of the Monastery and Chapel at Betharram.

Stained glass window in the ceiling of St. Michael's Chapel.

View of the River Gave, the Monastery,
the College of Notre Dame,
the Stations of the Cross
and the farm at Betharram.

The Chapel of the
Resurrection.
The 15th Station of the Cross.

refs to the trials of that time:

My hope is for a happy new year after this one of contradictions, per-
secutions, and heavy crosses etc., etc..

With faith and vision, he persevered and arranged for boarders to be accommodated in a rented house in the nearby village of Lestelle, but for a time was obliged to send his Latin pupils to other schools for whom he sometimes found the fees, and with much difficulty paid for Fr Barbe to study for his teaching certificate at Oloron. All this was in addition to his direction of the Community and the chaplaincy of the Shrine and the Convent.

In 1840, he was very disturbed by news that M Elicabide, whom he had warned about his greed for money, had murdered a wealthy widow of Pau and her two children for her money. He was awaiting trial in Bourdeaux. A letter to the Superior General of the Daughters of the Cross, Fr Taury, shows how distraught Fr Garicoits was. His letter describes the deep anguish he suffered while trying to reconcile Elicabide, whom he had taught as a former seminarist at Betharram, with his earlier faith.

I have received your kind letter just at the right moment. I deeply appreciate your heartfelt sympathy which has consoled me very much and helped dispel fears and worries constantly afflicting me. It has made a very powerful contribution to my peace of mind. Nothing has so upset me as those murders by the wretched E ....

I have tried to summon up common sense and faith, but nothing helped to deliver me from these ghastly feelings which have given me sleepless nights and which did not even leave me at the altar. Believe it or not, I could not even master my weakness enough to get a good night's sleep even in the peaceful rooms at Igon. That is the state I am in.

Today, I am looking more calmly at this dreadful business, which will do no good to our school. I am afraid that I will have to appear at the Assizes in Bourdeaux. Whatever God wishes will happen.

He appeared there before a commission to be interrogated on 10 Sept. 1840. Elizabide was found guilty and went to the guillotine. Witnesses say that he knelt down and prayed before going to the block.

Michael consoles himself with his own call to the religious life.

Alas! .... what grounds are here to detach ourselves from this world and attach ourselves to God.

In spite of crosses in its painful foundation, Notre Dame was a model Christian school and Catholics in other towns began to ask the Bishop for the Society to open schools in their towns. Vocations were increasing and Bishop Lacroix favoured this work.

In accord with your Excellency's intentions, M Hayet has been to Mauleon, and returned this week. He is waiting for the dossier that will enable him to clear things with the Rector of the Academie. They would like to include the letter that you kindly promised to the authorities in Mauleon. Jean Hayet, at twenty-nine, one year professed, and a subdeacon, was chosen as Founder and Headmaster of this College of St Francis. The dossier referred to in the letter was legally required for the opening of a school. It consisted of a statement by the Director of the School to the Mayor indicating the building designated for the school; one copy going to the Prefect and another to the Procurator General of the Department, a written reply and agreement of the Prefect and Procurator, the Birth certificate of the Headmaster, and a letter of compliance to the State from the Bishop. After this was submitted to the Rector of the Academie, the school would open one month after this process. There were delays and the Dossier was only returned to M Hayet on the 5th Dec., which held back the opening till 1850.

This delay was not foreseen and had to be borne with some pain and patience.

In the same month of November and the same year of 1849, St Michael opened the Catholic School at Orthez, another town in the region of the Bearn and Diocese of Bayonne.

There was a problem here. St Michael was not aware that the Dean and several parish priests had told parents that those who could not afford to pay for their education would receive it free. This posed quite a problem since this was the only means of revenue for the Society and the teachers.

Unaware of this, they set out from Betharram with great faith: one priest; Fr Barbe, the headmaster; a student, Jean Espagnolle, later ordained; and two brothers: Br Joannes who was professed and Arnaud Arbehere, a

First school of Notre Dame in Lestelle-Betharram.

View of the College of Notre Dame and the Monastery and Calvary.

teacher not professed; and Fr Garicoits. They were carrying the few goods they had by cart. When they arrived,the place was empty; they had nothing. Br Joanne knocked at the nearest door, a Protestant House. They gave them a blanket and some plates, glasses and forks. That night, they bought something from the nearby inn.

No sooner had we packed the luggage of Frs. Barbe and Espagnolle and the Brothers, writes Michael Garicoits, *than I went with them to Orthez where we are today. M Barbe has not been able to see the Mayor, but we have heard that he is delighted to see the school established. It appears that the Archpriest wants free schooling for the poor. This as a rule presents difficulties; to make it known publicly that schooling will be given without payment for those who cannot afford to pay, will prove rather embarrassing since we can only live by this means. As well as this, might not the well-off families from whom we would obtain some assistance feel humiliated to see their children confused with the children of the poorer classes? It would perhaps be better to set a modest charge, without giving the impression of our preference for the poor? We will carry out what your Excellency decides, and hope that we can implement it without delay because the parents are anxious to see the school open.*

Fr Garicoits kept a very close interest in this first foundation outside Betharram.

In 1852 there were two schools; the College of St Francis, the Secondary, and the College of Moncade, a primary. Fr Garicoits was acting on behalf of the Bishop in the material development of both schools.

He writes to Fr Pierre Barbe, headmaster of Moncade in 1852. At twenty-eight, he was the first headmaster and founder of the college, with Fr H. Serres as assistant. Fr Perguilhem was Superior of the primary school in name, but in fact the school was administered and run by Fr Barbe. Small in stature, he had a tenacious will and a firm hand, a smiling and friendly face. A keen overseer of the distribution of work, responsibilities of the staff, and exercises of piety. His intensive work bore fruitful results. He began the baccalaureate class and built a chapel which attracted the local people.

Fr Garicoits was responsible for detailed reports to the Bishop and precise implementation of his wishes, but he never lost sight in all this material pressure of the spiritual dimension of this foundation.

Here are the answers and the formal wishes of His Lordship in regard to the matters I have asked about.

Make a plan of and give an estimate of the new classrooms, the floors and steps leading to them etc.... use the plan and estimates given by the town's architect. I have told him that I will send these to him as soon as I receive them from you.

Tell Fr. Mazaris especially that if he has some spare moments, he can devise a course of solid Christian instruction and when he has composed it he can send me each one on completion so that I can make any revisions. You can say the same to Fr. Serres and others who are composing courses.

Monsignor has promised to write to M Plante as soon as he returns from his travels. Let me know about his return to Orthez without delay, and send me the plan and the estimate....

He was rather meticulous in seeing that accounts were kept; but in no way differing from those required in the world at large.

You will record in an exercise book both the amount that I gave you from the time of my arrival and the prescriptions of the Bishop that I have told you today, which I am afraid I have not seen carried out to the letter. These are dictated in the first place by common sense and by a proper understanding of these circumstances.

Although his letters are quite down to earth and are sprinkled with common sense, he never forgot their call to the religious life, which was to be apostles of the Sacred Heart:

Let no one fail to implement and understand these things, while, at the same time, putting into practice boundless charity within the limits of their position. The greater glory of God is here. When you do not keep to these boundaries, you inevitably make blunders. You may call them pious ones, if you wish, but always blunders, causing a reversal of standards. All these things create a fine spectacle which makes some apostles seem like children.

He expected high standards and that they were called to be credible witnesses of the Gospel. Yet he was no military general in his relationship with each member. His affection for those of his religious family was always real, comforting and reassuring as this letter conveys:

I embrace you, with all my heart, all the Priests and Brothers.

May the Spirit of Our Lord be your guide.... forever! Try to send me in Pau my umbrella and a dozen knives that M Chirou ordered from M Cousy, as soon as possible.(letter 86)

There was great pressure from all the surrounding parishes for schools. St Michael was present at a meeting where the Bishop was being pressed by parents to open a school at Asson. On that occasion, Fr Sarthy, a sickly person, passed by. St Michael turned to him and said; 'You will go. It is necessary to be dedicated and to sacrifice yourself. If you are ill, they will look after you.'

He replied very simply, 'Fiat . Fiat'. (Let it be done)

'What a difficult situation you have got me out of,' replied the Bishop.

Fr Sarthy with two Brothers, the schoolmaster Marie Pujo and Br Joannes, set out in November in a cart with whatever furniture they had and began preparing the place which consisted of one hall and two rooms upstairs. They had to beg wood for a fire to cook something to eat. Without fuel it was bitterly cold; Br Joannes had to return to Betharram for lack of nourishment. On one occasion, they all returned. St Michael managed to find some money for their support. Soon people rallied round. In the following year the school swelled from 30 to 150 pupils. But Fr Sarthy had to return because of ill health. The Community as a whole was stretched to the limits, yet Fr Garicoits did not allow them to lose sight of the essential calls to prayer, fidelity to their rule, communication and spiritual support in their religious life.

In 1855, the Bishop asked Fr Garicoits to take over the well-known College of St Marie at Oloron, which had fallen on bad times. He sent his best qualified young priests and Religious; Fr Rossigneux, a late vocation, with high degrees from Paris, and Fr Minvielle as Headmaster. The saintly and young Fr Auguste Etchecopar was on the staff there for two years as professor of Literature; he made a great impact on the children. Before the Fathers' arrival, when people spoke about Oloron they would say 'Oloron, oh no!' but now 'St Marie's, oh yes!'

These schools caused Fr Garicoits immense work and worry, yet through the cross flowed a spirit of love that made faith in the good news of the Gospel a reality and a way of life that brought the Gospel values to generations of children. This advice given to a headmistress, Sr Jeanne-Sophie, Daughter of the Cross, sums up St Michael's ideal and that of the Society in their relations with youth:

You should have a genuine desire to create a lasting and affectionate respect in your children so that through their respect for you they will receive an invaluable disposition in helping them turn their hearts to God. This is so true. But how does one become respected and loved by the children? In four words: love them and respect them greatly; exert yourself on their behalf constantly; love and respect them personally; speak to them; instruct them, reward them, even correct them as one who loves and respects them. This is what Our Lord does, Who is our model.(Letter 46)

17. St Michael and the Brothers.

F r Garicoits discovered the desire for the religious life among those who were not called to be priests. He first experienced the value of such dedicated men when a Capuchin community of priests and brothers asked for shelter at Betharram in 1835, after being expelled from their monastery in Spain. Fr Garicoits persuaded Mgr D'Astros to allow his community to offer them hospitality. They had a strong contingent of Brothers who provided valuable material help in their Community. After they departed in 1837, the Brothers were missed, and the Missioners encouraged young postulants to enter the Society as Brothers. In time, St Michael replaced the lay domestics with Brothers and also associated them with the Apostolate. The Community doubled.

At first, several postulants came and went, but one, Br Arnaud Gaye, who had left his flocks of sheep, decided to stay. He had the desire and call to live a life of prayer and a wish to work with the Fathers of Betharram. His tasks were numerous, from supervisor of studies in school, to sacristan in the Chapel, and jack-of-all-trades. He often accompanied Fr Garicoits on journeys. On one occasion Sr Marthe had to tell Fr Garicoits that Arnaud was doing too much. He became a close companion of the founder and was at St Michael's bedside in his last hours on the nights of the 13th and 14th, 1863.

Under the spiritual guidance of Fr Garicoits and Fr Cassou, the numbers of Brothers grew between 1837 and 1847 to over twenty. Their presence at Betharram filled the founder with joy. He spent much time with them and formed them in the love of the Sacred Heart. The Bishop approved of this project. Their vocation was to give glory to God. In spite of any shortcomings, they were to grow in grace, to be instruments of holiness among the laity with whom they were in closer contact than the priests, besides affording invaluable material and administrative support to the priests who were working on missions or in schools.

At St Michael's death, there were ninety Brothers and one hundred and seven Priests. After 1837, when Fr Garicoits added education to missions, some Brothers became supervisors and others were teachers. Many generations of young people in France and South America witnessed the dedication and holiness of these men. St Michael kept a balance between the needs of the mission and the schools. Many were skilled in trades and crafts. St Michael encouraged them in their skills. Around him were farmers, gardeners, builders, millers, bakers, cooks, confectioners, masons, carpenters, cabinet makers, cobblers, weavers, tailors. The young were apprenticed to these Brothers who gave a Christian formation in those irreligious times. St Michael wanted to set up technical and agricultural centres, the peasant families were only too pleased to send their children to his schools. These Brothers passed on their skills and formed their souls. Helped by Fr Cassou, the novice-master, St Michael created a Community of Brothers distinct from the priests. They intended to form two Societies. He bought the Farm of St Marie for them. They had their Superior, their organizers, their rule of life, times of prayer, a recreation room at the foot of the chapel of St Louis, a common room, and a library.

They were divided into four groups. Firstly, those who were accepted after two years' noviciate and were in temporary vows; secondly, those professed after ten years of temporary vows and over thirty years of age; thirdly, those in the schools who were the supervisors or teachers; and fourthly, those who worked manually.

After two years' noviciate, they took the three vows and became temporary professed Brothers. St Michael made it easy to reach this stage, but he was more exacting in admitting them to full profession; it needed ten years' probation and being over thirty years of age. The Supervisors wore a voluminous black gown and were addressed as Mr, with their surname. The fourth category wore a smock and were addressed as Mr or Brother with their first name, eg. Monsieur Pujo, Monsieur Marc, Br Jerome. Even if their work was different the same spirit united them all:

How difficult it is to find good people to work in the kitchen. Pray that God might send us a Brother who can cook, a Brother to answer the door, a Brother who can make clothes etc..... as He has sent us a Brother Sacristan.

Ask the good Lord to bless us and our works.(Letter 19)

In 1847, they built a workshop for shoemaking and tailoring. At first, three principal Brothers were engaged, Brothers Arabehere, Marthe, and Pujo, but soon the trades expanded. They planned an orphanage, and an agricultural and industrial school, which never materialised.

As most of the Brothers came from peasant backgrounds, two farms were bought. Fr Garicoits had considerable difficulty from the opposition of certain members when he was trying to acquire a farm for them, although he was fully supported by the Bishop. A Parish Priest promised to give ten thousand francs for the farm but some of the Community publicly opposed buying it so that when St Michael announced this gift, the opposition upset the donor, who withdrew his promise. ' Scarcely had I opened my mouth,' St Michael records, 'than they began to voice objections without any authority, and against all rules of humility, obedience and discretion. He was very upset and withdrew.'

The second occasion also proved difficult. 'The same person,' St Michael adds, 'made an offer to purchase on behalf of the Congregation. When the time for payment came, he declared he could not honour it. Far from showing displeasure, I replied: 'God be praised.' Instead of upsetting him, this left him with a good impression; for later the same hand offered us a considerable amount.'

1846 was a year of great famine and financially very hard for the new Community. The potato blight ravaged France as in Ireland and caused a million deaths. Wheat was scarce and too expensive for the poor. Some priests begged those with wheat to help the starving. St Michael had to find food for thirty priests and twenty brothers as well as the boarders at Notre Dame. From 1840-1845, he put aside twenty thousand francs for the restoration of the Calvary, ten thousand francs for the purchase of the farm of St Marie, and paid for the opening of the secondary school at Notre Dame in Nov. 1847.

He relied on the generosity of benefactors and even more on Divine Providence. His faith never wavered. In one of these most difficult moments, he said: 'God has not abandoned us. Not only have we passed

St. Marie's farm today.

St. Marie's farm building, reconstructed by the Brothers in St. Michael's day.

through this dreadful winter, but even the money that we thought lost, has tided us over.' (Bourdenne p145)

He writes to a priest benefactor.

My Dear Friend,

I do not know how to thank you for your help. I was intending to come and see you to discuss all our business. I hope in one way or another to do this. In the mean time, a thousand thanks.

In regard to buying wheat, I believe we will have to wait and be content to purchase day by day, sack by sack, relying on what I receive and on what the good God sends.

In a month from now I will either see or write to you. In the meantime, if you find some hectolitres at a reasonable price, see about it. (Letter 45)

A bequest from a local family for a Mission every ten years at Coarraze secured funds for a farm, which he mentions in his letter to the Bishop.

This agreement will be entered in our registers along with the above sum of one thousand five hundred francs agreed for this purpose. This has served to purchase a little estate in the country at Montaut which we have acquired at the cost of one thousand five hundred francs.(Letter 38)

The farm known as Sainte Marie's, comprised a house and two barns about three kilometres from the Monastery. As they made their daily journey to and fro, usually on foot, the Brothers, carrying their implements, recited the Rosary.

Not long after its purchase, a meteorite struck the thatched roof of one of the buildings which was totally burnt and caused damage to the others.

That day, a Brother ran back to the Monastery and told St Michael that the Farm was burnt down.

His first words were: 'Was anyone hurt?'

The Brother replied: 'No one.'

'Thank God.'

He called the Brothers together. The carpenters and builders immediately set about rebuilding. With trowel in hand he worked with them.

One problem that caused Fr Garicoits some concern was the fact that as the Brothers belonged to a Diocesan Society unaffected by the Concordat with the Vatican, they did not qualify for exemption from military service. The Brothers of Christian Schools were attached to the University of France by an imperial decree in 1808 which exempted them from military service. The Law of 1845 exempted all Religious Orders from military service but the Society of the Sacred Heart was not at that time legally recognised.

St Michael to benefit from this exemption was trying to affiliate them to the Christian Brothers, but having no success there, he wrote for advice to Jersey in 1845, to Blessed Jean-Marie de la Mennais, founder of the Brothers of Christian Instruction.

Reverend Vicar General,

Your kindness in answering my confrere's inquiries has encouraged me to send you this letter, as I would appreciate your advice ....

I am the head of a society of missioners which includes Religious Brothers among whom are some who are able to teach. It would not be difficult for me to urge, even those others who apply to us in quite good numbers, to do the same, bearing in mind that we have a Primary School directed by a priest in our establishment. In this way, enough teaching Brothers would emerge prepared to combat to some degree the evils which the young teachers coming from the universities fail to destroy.

Everyone agrees with my project. For a long time, the Bishop has been urging me to implement it. There is one obstacle stopping me. Generally speaking, I realise that these young men being poor and also not qualifying for State Exemption will be subject to the law of conscription. Because of this, I am in danger of losing them after maintaining and training them for many years, just when they would start to be useful.

I am asking you, Reverend Vicar General, if you could advise me how I can overcome this problem. At first I thought of the possibility of affiliating them to the Brothers of Christian Schools; I have already received information on this point which has led me nowhere. Hence I have been advised to consult you. Would you please, for the greater glory of God, give me your views on this matter and advise me what means I should take to succeed in this enterprise, either in the way described above or in whatever way you think best to achieve the desired result. In a word, I would be grateful for all the information that your care and experience can provide.(Letter 33) It seems that this problem was not solved in his time.

Fr Garicoits knew each brother personally. Certain ones became well-known in those early days. Br Jerome Peyrous, although illiterate, left in his short time in noviciate a reputation of holiness and prayer. In spite of his illiteracy, his conversation uplifted those who were close to him. Br Joannes Arosteguy, formerly sacristan at Bayonne Cathedral, took his share of the hardships and deprivations in many foundations, including those at Orthez, Pau, Asson, San Jose, and Montevideo. Br Pierre Quilhahauquy, secretary for St Michael, being very close to him in life, worked with Fr Etchecopar for the process of canonization. Jean-Baptiste Cariton was an authority in the cultivation of the grape and the process of making wine. Br Firmin, a tireless builder, restored the farm of Sainte Marie, built the noviciate and the College, etc... Br Jean-Marie Pujo built and sculpted the chapels that housed the Stations of the Cross.

The Brothers were like a central artery of the Society, which was strengthened by their prayers just as much as by their work. It seemed that in those painful times when the Bishop was ignoring the very existence of the Society in Betharram, the Brothers remained faithful to the holiness of that revered place and stood as true witnesses to the reality of Religious Life. Although one might consider the world of St Michael to be patronising and at variance with the equality expected in our times, St Michael was inevitably a man of his times, yet by creating a way of Religious Life for men who were willing to commit themselves entirely to God, he was in advance of those times. They were not priests, but truly and indispensably called to the values of the Kingdom in their various capacities: by teaching, by administration or by the work of their hands. It was essentially not what they did, but who they were that really mattered; men called to follow Christ without reserve, without delay and without any if's and but's.

Feature of the door to St. Marie's farm, made by the brothers.

72

18. Joys and Sorrows

B y reading his letters one sees how St Michael tried to bring out the best in whoever he was dealing with: in priests, brothers, sisters, lay-people and children. As he led them to Christ, he strongly emphasised working together as a community while not neglecting to hold a deep respect for individuals. To avoid disorder and mismanagement, he directed that those with responsibilities keep to the limits of their duties and not interfere with those of others, yet he always urged them to put into practice the limitlessness of love. His letters to priest-headmasters in those disordered times demanded obedience to the bishop and superiors while asking members to work in unity of purpose.

He often wrote to encourage superiors to support and develop their members' abilities and sometimes gave a summary of their qualities and weaknesses, yet always encouraged a positive approach. *'Take men as they are and try to turn all to good account,' he wrote to Didace Barbe, Superior of St Jose, Buenos Aires. (490)*

His letters reveal that he had many difficulties among his own communities. He began with five companions. One of them, Fr Guimon, later in Argentina, became quite independent of the Bishop and his Superior and was the subject of concern, as indicated in his letters to Fr Barbe.

Although all schools were under the Bishop, St Michael was the Superior of the communities that ran them; this proved a source of strength at times and a cause of conflict at others. Problems in foundations in making numbers viable from year to year caused at first some hardship in the communities; numbers vacillated from seventy to twenty-seven in Moncade, from five to one hundred in Buenos Aires. There were problems with staff.

Michael had to sack the Headmaster at Betharram for charging pupils to supplement his salary without Fr Garicoit's consent. Many parents who appreciated the academic development under this headmaster were very angry with his decision and threatened to withdraw pupils. Fr Michael had warned Elicabide of his excessive desire for money and had said quite prophetically that 'it would lead him to the gallows.' His decision proved to be justified by later events. The switching of staff from primary to secondary schools by headmasters at the expense of the former in Orthez was a matter of concern; other concerns were the eccentric behaviour of some priest teachers, disagreements between members and St Michael, and in some cases, defections of very talented priests. A contributory cause was the Bishop's attitude towards members taking vows of obedience and poverty. Since he did not believe that the Society should be committed in this way, there was always the problem of stability and permanence as a community. Members could be released from the Society through the Bishop. St Michael had the painful experience of seeing their departure.

These included Jean Espagnolle, a brilliant classics scholar and former novice master; Florent Lapatz, another acclaimed teacher in rhetoric at Oloron; Dominique Guilha, former Headmaster at Moncade; Jean Hayet, a former Superior at Oloron; and Victor Paradis who joined the Holy Ghost Fathers in 1868.

Another concern at that time was Fr Minvielle's treatment of Junior Seminarists for the Society who were studying at Oloron. St Michael decided that it would be better to send them home while he found some room for them at the school in Betharram.

The care and attention as well as practical advice that he gave was a definite spur to many.

As one who seeks for treasures both old and new, his strength in conflict was drawn either from God's Word in Scripture, or from the Fathers of the Church and from well-known writers on spirituality like Suarez and Vincent de Paul, as well as the spiritual writers of his day. His letters of advice not only demonstrate his knowledge, but his tireless efforts in creating an identity for Religious Life that each member of the Society was able to follow. The variety of situations and the variety of needs that he deals with show not only his knowledge, but his faith and wisdom in challenging others to move forward in the varied and demanding situations of their lives.

Some of St Michael's most carefully and often affectionately penned letters were to people that failed in one way or another to heed his advice, either by leaving the Society or by not implementing particular requests. A letter written to a member of the Society, Florent Lapatz, a graduate in classics, teaching at the College of Moncade, shows St Michael's care and concern even for those who opposed him. This priest had become so infatuated with the classics and the pagan atmosphere of the universities that he changed his name to a Greek one, but there were other matters that needed changing in his life. St Michael's Latin quotations in this letter are translated in bold print: .

Let me speak to you quite frankly. I am always pleased to hear about your success in literary achievements. The more you know, the more you will be ready to employ yourself usefully in training and helping others to advance in holiness.

*Firstly, you should **attend to God** and the law of charity which He has engraved in the soul: then you can pay attention to Literature and Sciences, which, in themselves, are neither a positive nor negative means for salvation, and only serve our needs in so far as they conform to the dispositions of Providence.*

*I am afraid that there is a lack of order within yourself: it is because you are ignoring the real object of your life and putting the means in place of it. You are saying to yourself, **'Blessed are those who possess these good things,'** instead of proclaiming before God and men, **'Blessed are those who have God as their master. My happiness is to cling to God.'***

The sciences, literature and theology must be servants not masters; they must follow and not lead.(St John Chrysostom de Sacer Bk 1). Gifted people who indulge in studies, unworthy of themselves, and those with serious responsibilities who engage in pleasure and empty pursuits, are an utter disgrace....What is a priestly heart, but an Ark of the Covenant, where lies the tablets of the Law, because he reveres spiritual doctrine(ibid)?"

What are then the attainments in which the priest should excel? Certainly, there are those which help him fulfil perfectly all his duties as a man of God and a minister of Jesus Christ, but, in no way, do those help, whose object is to create an effect and to pander to curiosity. These pursuits are quite acceptable for transitory things, but, in a way, regrettable for those things which are not. What is more harmful, may I ask, more wicked, when a priest knows perfectly **"pointless philosophical discussions and knowledge which is not knowledge at all,'** *(1Tim6;20) while he is ignorant of the writings of the Apostles, and the name and number of the books of Scripture.*

'Now daily we see priests giving up the Gospels and prophets to read comedies'.*(Jerome Ad Nepos.)*

Is my intention to limit your enthusiasm, to confine your talents? Not at all. **'An educated man needs to know as much as possible, but he should leave what is vain, to those who are vain . Everything within yourself should be in order .Your conversation should be tested by Holy Writ or by the Fathers; by Tertulian or Cyprian, etc.. By commitment to reading and daily meditation, make your heart into a library of Christ. Amen'** *(ibid.)*

Read Chapter 43 of the third book of the **Imitation of Christ** *and believe me*

Yours sincerely in the Lord (Letter 241)

Towards the end of his life, St Michael had considerable difficulty with the schools. Here is a letter to Fr Angelin Minvielle, Superior of the Seminary at D'Oloron. We note how St Michael sees through appearances and grasps the realities of situations.

I have been charmed with peace and joy, but I am very much afraid that this is not the peace of the Lord: that lasting and eternal peace which alone is desirable; or is it that Divine charity, the first and precious fruit for which each of us should pray during these forty days of special prayer for our poor Community. We must ask to find peace by just doing the good pleasure of God.

I feel deeply hurt by the way our members have publicly opposed a

Superior, whatever he is like, sent by those appointed by the Bishop. Where will this spirit lead? It will make any religious society impossible to run! Every religious society is a union of men governed by other men, with all their human failings, yet, who are put there for them as representatives of God. Do we always have to be slow of heart to believe and to embrace the Will of God, (Lk 24;25) and when it is shown to us so slow to place our trust and happiness in it ?

Do you need to find some superior angel to replace Fr. Hayet? I deplore this spirit which would find a Seraphim far more unbearable than Fr. Hayet because a Seraphim would be a friend of order, obedience, humility and charity etc., and would not tolerate that spirit of accepting only what suits them. (Letter 603)

In his correspondence are very affectionate letters sometimes written to various Daughters of the Cross whose families he knew. Almost always he encouraged them in their vocation, and never presumed that they would always be faithful to their calling. He understood that Religious could fall and fail, even when vocations were plentiful, and are always in need of encouragement and guidance.

While St Michael was attending the 'Great Assembly' at La Puye, the Mother House of the Daughters of the Cross in Central France, he would hear the latest news of various Sisters in convents throughout France. On the occasion of this letter, he writes to a sister whose family he knows very well, but he also is aware that she is having difficulties in her vocation even though she has been in the Order for many years. His advice for her is to become 'little, humble... and persevering' and to remain happy and at peace. In the culture of that era, he was appealing to the commonly accepted role expected of all respectable women: daughters to be submissive to their parents, wives to their husbands and nuns to be obedient to the Church. In order to win approval, women were in general required to keep to a decision, rather than reverse it. St Michael used these expectations, but he also believed that faithfulness to the 'grace of God, would enable a sister keep her 'precious vocation'.'

My Dear Sister,

I received your letter on time; unfortunately I did not find out about your dear Father, as I was engaged at the Great Assembly. I sincerely hope that the Good God will keep him with us for many years to come.

I thank God with all my heart for bringing you back to your old and very good Superior. I like to persuade myself that by the grace of God , He will make you each day more faithful to your holy and precious vocation without examining if it is real. Is looking back pleasing to God, after so many years?..... Go on..... This is fear...... How horrid!

Be always little, submissive, happy, content, and persevering. Amen, amen..

Then you will not fail to be eternally a crowned queen (Reine); halabiz. Aincina beraz eta ...... etc(a long list of exhortations in Basque follows to the end of the letter)..

"So be it. Go forward. Never look back even in self-appraisal. There is no doubt that the Good God wants you for Himself. I must write two words to your sister. She is very good. May you also be as good and happy as she is. Adieu, my child, pray for us. I now write little, but I pray every day. Do the same for me.

Letter 347   To Sr Reine... 27th Dec. 1861...

He encouraged letters from his own members and from Religious associated with him, especially the Daughters of the Cross whom he had helped in their spiritual formation; in fact, he seems open to all. Many of his letters give encouragement and advice.(348)

The following letter is written to a young Basque postulant whom he has not met. She has written for advice. He encourages her to believe that in spite of the inadequacies she feels, she is loved very much by God, and that in spite of the difficulties she experiences in her work, she is in fact doing 'His very special work.' He sees in her some lovely qualities and encourages her to develop them. He asks her to acquire openness of heart which seems to mean trusting in herself and in her gifts, because they come from God, so persuading her to use and share them. He always insists that she develops a great trust in God in spite of insurmountable problems that she feels within her own character and behaviour. To overcome these obstacles, he encourages her to go to the source of Love by frequent Communion. The more the temptation, the more frequent the Communion.

At work, she seems to be hearing conversation that she finds sinful and upsetting. Being of a sensitive disposition she seems to blame herself and feels guilty for either not attempting to stop it directly or for not objecting to it. St Michael advises her not to attempt what may well be impossible, and only to effect change if it is possible. Even when she feels soiled or maybe depressed, by what she has heard, she should still go to Communion; 'she should not be drawn away from Jesus.'

Once again his regular advice is, 'Go forward.'

I take a spare moment to answer your letter. I will first of all say that your good letter is a very pleasant surprise for I do not know you. Everything tells me that by the grace of God you will do much good there. But I ask you to please listen to me;

1. *You can be assured of my prayers such as they are.*

2. *You must open your heart to the thought that you are truly the well-beloved child of your heavenly Father in spite of external and internal difficulties, that you are continually doing His very special work, and are always in His sight, always assisted by Him with very great favours, the object of His unfailing attention. All this is certain and asks on your part the greatest openness of heart, the most complete surrender, humility, thankfulness, tranquility, joy and inner and outward peace which nothing should ever change. Such a good Father, such a Friend guides us; so what else do we need?*

(Letter 348   To Sr Sophie Flavie. Igon 27 Dec. 1861)

Many young women entered religious life through his direction and were helped to remain faithful to their calling. With some of these, a very close friendship evolved. Such a one was Sister Jerome. Her original name was Dominique Pedechar from Bagnere de Bigorre, the first postulant from this area to enter after the foundation by St Elizabeth Bichier Des Ages at Igon, in 1826. She became Superior of many communities and was a Sister of 'outstanding calibre'; a great administrator, organizer, and solver of difficulties. St Michael appreciated her exceptional gifts. His letters convey much respect, and from their frequency indicate a deep friendship. They are written in a relaxed and familiar style. When she was at Igon, he enjoyed speaking with her; both she and he confided in each other; both seemed kindred spirits. St Michael appreciated and sought her advice, even in matters that were secret and delicate, such as the possible amalgamation of the Society of the Holy Cross with Betharram. Although she was very involved in temporal affairs, deep down in her heart she sought a life of recollection and prayer. St Michael knew this and had similar feelings himself, arising from his own situation. In spite of her remarkable talents, she was beset with scruples which were the result of a Jansenist upbringing. Being on friendly terms, St Michael occasionally wrote in a humorous vein in his letters to help her come to terms with her fears, by referring to them as the 'old madwoman'. She was wise enough to know what he meant.

Another was Sister Sabinien, formerly Marie Peyrou, born at Ossun in 1825. She owed her vocation to St Michael whom she consulted at 19, and continued to seek his counsel in her noviciate from 1846-8 and as a professed Sister from 1859 until his death in 1863. She became Superior General from 1859 to 98. She opened thirty-one houses and took the number from 2,599 Religious in the order to 2,773. At the process of St Michael's canonization, she said: 'It is incredible how Fr Garicoits in spite of so many other commitments, had worked for so many years to form our novices, to instruct and support our Professed in the practice of virtue, and to engender among them a deep love for the Lord and the poor, a spirit of zeal, of simplicity, of self-sacrifice, detachment from the world, which our own founders sought to instill. She died at La Puye in 1898. Here is an extract from a letter written in 1849.

My Dear Sister,

You are not mistaken in thinking that I do not forget the Daughters of the Cross, even though they are so far away and I have not seen them for a long time. One cannot think otherwise, if you understand the respect and devotion I have for your Congregation.

Yes, my dear Sister, I have followed their cart in spirit from district to district, the cart that finally put you down at Ustaritz. When I learnt the important post that you had to take up there, I said as you did: God be praised. I am so pleased to think that you were so well disposed to undertake the responsibilities of this new position, relying only on the special graces that the good Lord has reserved for you.

Continue also to love your Sisters and always behave towards them in such a way as to inspire their affection for you, using this only as a means of bringing them more effectively to God. In this way you will bring about your own salvation along with that of many others. Amen..

Last Thursday, I visited the Sisters at Benejacq. It is a new residence which they have founded. They are loved there very much. Particularly my dear Sr Theodora is so changed, learned etc... But what is better in my eyes is that this dear Sister is no longer sad, takes things cheerfully, and I think, is in good spirits.... I hope that she will be a very good Daughter of the Cross. Write to encourage her, speak to her from the fullness of your heart, the heart of a warrior, with confidence in God and in the graces of the Congregation which considers as being of very, very small account the crosses allowed by Providence. (Letter 62)

No doubt the recipients treasured these letters and drew from them inspiration and renewal when they re-read them. When he wrote,he must have given them much joy as well as a genuine uplift.

'I love you all,' he sometimes concludes, 'especially the Eskualdunas (Basques) in Jesus Christ.' (347)

In the following letter to a Sister Theodorine, he not only expresses his happiness in hearing of how she feels in efforts to create true community life, but joyfully confirms the qualities she needs to attain it: *'It always gives me renewed joy when I see thankful, happy, and reliable persons in God's service.'* His insight enabled him to advise and encourage her because he had that rare gift of discernment which sees that even the good and faithful need support and upbuilding in their vocation; for they too can drop away.

In this letter he seems to be very much in touch with laypeople: with families and friends known to the sisters. He had that quality that enabled him to feel their joys, their hopes, and their fears.

He does not fail to remember to ask for prayers for a good and holy end to life when someone is gravely ill and has no hope of recovery. He did not assume, as sometimes happens in practice, that the sick automatically reach a good end.

He does not utter platitudes, but looks beyond this life: 'She will be saved.'

353 To Sr Theodorine, Daughter of the Cross

Betharram. 12 Feb. 1862.

My Good Sister,

1. *I received your kind letter over a month ago. It is always with renewed pleasure that I see thankful, happy, and reliable persons in God's service. Oh! I pray with all my heart that you always keep these sentiments. There is nothing more true than these dispositions so that you will walk in a manner worthy of your holy and precious vocation and make yourself always more pleasing in the eyes of the Lord.*

2. *Undoubtedly it is not brilliant here, especially when you think of what you have seen elsewhere. Poor John, they say, is always the same; the sister-in-law is ill. It is distressing, as you say, but God permits it. Have patience and pray so that all has an end that results in a complete Christian life. Let us join our prayers with those who are already in heaven.*

Let us pray also for Therese, I had not seen her for a long time. The other day I met her at the Peyrounats. She seemed well. For her there is nothing to say except that she always has her own ideas and that she is always a little fussy. Otherwise she is good; for that she will be saved.

Brigitte Fontarabie, sister of Philippine Perounat, died this week. Farewell, dear Sister, I leave you for the time being and wish you a happy new year. Pray for us.

Being the Superior of the schools run on behalf of the Diocese, St Michael would naturally have known many parents who were active in their support and who were in positions of responsibility in the town. On this occasion he is responding to a regular pilgrim to Betharram who had a particular regard for Honore Serre, priest and former headmaster of the school at Orthez.

One can see how St Michael, although writing in the formal manner of those times, shows his interest in the spiritual life of this family.

Madam

I only received your letter on my return from Bayonne, which explains the delay in my response. I see no reason why I should be away during the time you mention. We shall be able to spend time on your proposals when you make your pilgrimage.

I will carefully look after the notebook that you mention in your letter as well as all the belongings of our much loved deceased.(Honore Serres)

I heard from the Bishop's secretariat of Adrien's article published in Fr Serre's memory. Besides the general sorrow that this article recalls, we are very moved by his sentiments and the way they were expressed. I have seen some in tears while it was read. Oh, how touching on the part of such a student towards such a master.......

I most sincerely wish that these sentiments grow in Adrien for his own happiness and for yours.

I am, with profound respect, your very humble and obedient servant.

Letter 246   Madam Raymond Plante. Betharram   1 Mar 1860

Her son Adrien Plante was magistrate and mayor of Orthez, and later Deputy of the Basse Pyrenees.

The letters give us a glimpse of St Michael's spirituality and attitude towards the laity; they reveal someone that not only Religious, but all Christians can adopt in their search to follow in the footsteps of Christ.

19. Formation of Members in the Religious Life

L ike a plant the Society grew slowly: the soil that formed it, was not only the providential circumstances that brought it into existence, but also the structures gradually and painfully created for the future through the care of the founder. The first members adopted the rules of the Hasparren Missioners of the Sacred Heart, but St Michael's inspiration urged him to search for a way of religious life that would conform to what he believed was God's plan for the Society. His perceptions, his faith, and experience in studying the various rules of Religious life and particularly that of the Jesuits which was closest to his inspiration, enabled the Society to develop a form of Religious Life that would endure after over half of Diocesan Societies disappeared.

From the beginning Fr Garicoits made every effort to form the members according to their pastoral work and did not fail to use every means of communication to make them aware and informed in the knowledge and practice of their responsibilities.

He himself taught the young students Philosophy and Theology and never delegated this very important and critical responsibility to anyone else. He may well have believed that in this way he was called to create an ideology that would include and heighten these important and essential studies in the Society's future development.

Those who were to be missioners were the object of his particular attention. He had a group of priests who would examine their sermons and instructions in regard to subject matter, delivery, presence, and even gestures. This followed the good practice of well-known Congregations like the Redemptorists. He composed methods for giving spiritual exercises and detailed rules on the distribution of sermons, commentaries, and various liturgies, not forgetting wise advice about conduct towards the Parish clergy and faithful.

He did the same in regard to those in schools concerning their relationship with pupils in class and in the study, with their parents and with other teachers, and with their superiors. He tried to communicate clearly how they were expected to behave. At the centre of all these details was the spirituality of the heart in practicing the limitlessness of Love. He created opportunities for ongoing formation in the spiritual lives of the various groups. Even a few days before he died, he was planning a week's renewal through the Exercises of St Ignatius for all the Missioners.

The Brothers were not forgotten. He taught them ways of prayer; how to meditate, and to overcome their faults. 'My Friends, realise that you are not working as servants, but are Religious; not slaves but brothers. Here you do not work from fear, but from love. For you have come here, not from a spirit of fear, but from the Spirit of love.'

He encouraged them in their work and often worked with them. One saw him laying the table and doing the washing up with them. Sometimes he did the more unpleasant jobs too.

His daily routine

He got up at 4.00 am, sometimes earlier. He spent at least an hour in prayer. He walked to Igon in his first years, later he rode a horse or went by carriage. He led the Sisters in meditation, celebrated Mass, and heard confessions, then he returned to Betharram, usually without breakfast. On his return he took a cup of chocolate,then he taught Philosophy and Theology to the students for the priesthood which any priests present in the house usually attended. These lessons were always of interest and were spiced with familiar and helpful anecdotes while at the same time conveying deep truths of Theology. Sometimes there was a friendly sharing of experiences between Fr Garicoits, the missionaries and others.

After this the Community took lunch, but Fr Garicoits often remained at his desk, catching up on correspondence for spiritual direction or business, preparing conferences, working on the constitution and rules, studying spiritual writers or philosophers, or writing up notes.

He found time to pray, to hear confessions of those within and outside the Community, to help children in the school with their studies, and some, whom he thought had vocations to the priesthood, with Latin.

At the end of the day, he took a meal with the Community, which took place in silence and with spiritual reading. After this, he spent some time in recreation with the Community, then he prayed the Divine Office and the rosary, and finally, after kneeling before the Cross, he retired to his room.

20. Conflict; fears and hopes

Just as it is said that the Church flowed from the pierced Heart of Christ, St Michael accepted that his call to bring a new Society into the Church needed a complete surrender of himself to God's plans, which included suffering. His model for Superiors or those in positions of responsibility was the Sacred Heart. Writing to a Daughter of the Cross who asked how she should act as Superior, he recalled how Jesus suffered from Peter's betrayal and yet was prepared to resolve His own hurt and Peter's shame through love and reconciliation. *'To govern with love is to create children,'* he wrote. *Jesus asked Peter: 'Do you love me?'....... When Peter assured Jesus that he did love Him, that made him ready for leadership: 'Feed My lambs.'*

St Michael did not falter in the face of opposition, but with great faith and trust used his great gifts of perception and courage to resolve and cope with conflict. Conflict was God's way of enriching his faith and deepening his wisdom; the Cross which was so ingrained in his spirituality, not only created in a providential way an identity among the members of the Society with the Sacred Heart, but gave them through the Cross, the very means of growth.

The most serious and sensitive conflict came from the difference between St Michael's conception of Religious Life and that of Bishop Lacroix: a clash of minds.... This difference with the Bishop over the nature of Religious Life and the very nature of the Society persisted till the end of St Michael's life. From the beginning he felt that he should found a Religious Order which would practise the three vows of Poverty, Chastity and Obedience. At first, the various Bishops envisaged a Community of Diocesan Missioners not committed to any vows; some of the early members took the same view. Fr Garicoits saw these beginnings as only the first stage towards a Religious Congregation. At first he was not clear how this was to be realised. But he was clear in his own mind that he should follow the signs that Providence placed in front of him. Mgr D'Astros said: 'Do not forestall Providence, but follow all its signs with generosity and love.' This was the principle that he scrupulously followed in the gradual development and growth of the Society from its very modest beginnings.

In 1835, the Society was authorised to follow the Rule of the Hasparren Missioners. Fr Garicoits was elected Superior by his five companions, who promised to put all their possessions in common and obey him; this would be equivalent to the vows of poverty and obedience.

Fr Garicoits led the Community by word and example in this way of life. After his retreat at Toulouse with the Jesuits, he realised that their Constitutions and the life of St Ignatius fulfilled his vision. From that time, he and his companions studied and began to live according to that spirit by following these constitutions.

In 1838, Bishop Lacroix was appointed to Bayonne. Fr Garicoits went to ask his permission for them to live by these rules. He allowed this but said that he would in due course provide them with constitutions himself. Three years later, in 1841, he gave them their new constitutions. To their utter astonishment Mgr Lacroix proposed a form of life without vows of any kind. For them, it was a return to the past. At the repeated request of Fr Guimon, he allowed them to take vows. In effect these constitutions were quite contrary to the vision of St Michael for their Religious Life. The Superior was to be appointed by the Bishop and not by the Community.The Bishop reserved the right to appoint members to main posts and missions. Those who had been permitted to take perpetual vows would be dispensed if they were no longer part of the Society, for whatever reason. There could be no question of seeking approbation from the Holy See.

No one could tell the pain this caused Fr Garicoits, as, out of deference to authority, he did not discuss it. He was in a very difficult and sensitive position; on the one hand, he was to remain faithful to his inspiration and on the other, to remain faithful to his Bishop. He firmly believed in the Holy Spirit Who drove him forward to keep the Society together, to carry out God's work and to find ways and means of reconciling these positions. He came to the belief that he should submit to the Bishop for the present, but should never allow anyone to obscure his vision, and that he should work with boundless trust in God for the future, in so far as obedience permitted. He faithfully accepted the Bishop's constitutions, but regarded them as a minimum of perfection, and did not fail to teach a higher ideal to his own members. He believed that sooner or later, Divine Providence would present a favourable moment for the Society to present his project to the Bishop. Fr Garicoits taught that God's greater glory would be served by these trials. Fr Barbe in his testimony said, 'Fr Garicoits went forward with his divine inspiration while obeying the will and authority of the Bishop. He suffered much, since some members agreed with the Bishop's ideas. He had to use considerable discretion and unenviable prudence.' Here are some of Fr Garicoit's thoughts confided to a Sister Superior, arising, no doubt, from his own experience.

There is often more good in accepting the task of showing authority than in refusing to do what you feel is right. There is sometimes as little humility in believing oneself important enough to be able to hinder God's work, as there is in giving yourself the credit for its success.

If God is with you, all will be well; yet not without effort, difficulty and suffering.

To rule, that is through love, is to bear children.... Religious Superiors are mothers. Children do not come without suffering; in this situation pain is more than a felt condition, it might be seen as the enabler. In any case, it is inevitable; but ultimately, I repeat, if God is with you, all will be well. (Letter 41)

The Community lived for ten years under these constitutions. Fr Garicoits repeated more and more frequently that these constitutions were inadequate and ruinous as regards stable community life. He felt the need among other things for the authority of the Superior over the Community to be broadened. But how could he discuss this in a way which would persuade Mgr Lacroix to accept important modifications? Could he hope for even a partial review? He felt that he had to try.

He had a number of painful meetings with the Bishop. On one occasion, returning from Bayonne, he remarked, 'How painful it is to bring a congregation to birth!'

He studied the lives of St Ignatius and his companions, especially when they went to Rome to present their plan of life to the Pope. Fr Garicoits wrote a new constitution with amendments which he considered necessary, yet taking into account the thoughts and intentions of the Bishop. He hoped to present it to him when the providential moment arrived. Most of his companions were of the same mind. Fr D. Barbe submitted for approval a way of life along the lines of St Michael. It could be summed up thus:

1. That the life of the Society or Family of the Sacred Heart should be governed by the Superior.

2. The Society's work in the Diocese and in public should be regulated by the Bishop.

In 1851, at a general assembly, the Bishop conceded that the Society could live by the constitutions of the Society of Jesus where these did not disagree with his own, and that they could elect a Superior that met with his approval. Two commissions were set up: one to look at material needs, the other to consider the vows and the way various members observed life in the Society. From this time, other concessions were obtained.

Another action of the Bishop which caused pain, was the creation of a Society of his own, in opposition to Betharram: the Society of Higher Studies, the Priests of the Holy Cross at Oloron.

Joseph Menjoulet, Vicar General, formerly director and professor of moral theology at Bayonne, was appointed founder of the Society of Higher Studies. He was a learned man who wrote extensively on local Church history, including a Chronicle of the Sanctuary at Betharram. The enterprise of Fr Menjoulet, in fact of Mgr Lacroix, was short-lived. One may recall that St Michael began his foundation with the approval of the former Bishops, Mgr D'Astros and Mgr d'Arbou. The new Bishop initially had other plans for Fr Garicoits. He thought that Betharram, being on the edge of the Diocese, was badly situated as a house of formation and education. As a member of the Society of St Sulpice, a community of priests without religious vows, he favoured the same for his Diocesan Missioners. St Michael wanted a Religious Society with vows modelled on the Jesuits. After six months, the Bishop intended removing St Michael from Betharram and appointing him as rector of the Seminary in Bayonne. Because of a public outcry and an interview with St Michael, who humbly presented his reasons for staying at Betharram, in fact kneeling before the Bishop as he did so, the Bishop changed his plans. However, he transferred the work of Betharram to Holy Cross and indirectly made people know that he wanted Fr Garicoïts at Holy Cross. St Michael held to his principle which was, 'To do the will of God where one finds oneself, without interfering in anything else.' Without taking notice of rumours, he pressed ahead. 'God has called me to Betharram,' he would say, 'for that reason I have stayed. People speak of the Holy Cross at Oloron; I am always ready to obey the orders of the Bishop.'

The Bishop's orders never came. St Michael loyally supported the new foundation of Holy Cross. During this period, he did not search so much for vocations, fearing that this would upset the Bishop. However, after an enthusiastic start, the Society never rose above twelve members, and gradually began to decline, as several left; the way of life proposed by the Bishop, which the Society of Betharram could not accept, did not work at Oloron. The founder eventually turned to Betharram and asked for amalgamation in 1852. From this time, Mgr Lacroix became more supportive of Betharram. From then on, St Michael intensified his search for vocations which doubled from thirty to sixty in five years. His delight is evident in this letter which refers to a favourable meeting with the Bishop.

I have not forgotten and will not forget your heartening words when as a Bishop you had the kindness to say to me some time ago that I was to contact you: 'We need vocations. You do not pray enough... Then pray that God sends them to us.'

This desire you expressed to me several times with the same enthusiasm: that you wished to see your projects grow. I recall particularly the occasion at Bayonne when you said, 'I would give permission for any candidate who wished to be part of the various works of Betharram. They would do their studies in theology there and I would shorten it to their needs.' Not long ago, Your Excellency repeated this at Betharram with the same generosity towards all those who wished to be part of this family.

*Here is a plan, Monsignor, which in the past I had thought of, it is true, as a means of fostering vocations and especially in the early formation of candidates in the spirit of the Society, which is a spirit of humility, charity, obedience and self-sacrifice. (**Const of the Soc. art 2**). However I had no call to propose it to your Excellency then, and I had in fact lost sight of it entirely since the start of Fr Menjoulet's enterprise.* (Letter 63) These requests were granted.

The question of amalgamation caused him much concern, as this letter indicates, written to one of his closest confidants, Sr Jerome. True to his deep faith, he requests prayers.

We must pray and ask for prayers so that our good Father continues to guide us and carry the weight of our ministries....

.... God for God and everything for God, or, indeed, nothing but for God, this is what I pray for both you and me; to do only and wholly the will of God. Yes, my dear Sister, especially at this moment it is what you should pray for and ask others to pray for concerning our little Society.

Since you want news of Betharram, I will tell you that this poor Society is possibly at a quite critical moment.

This is the situation which you must keep secret, since nobody knows

Auguste Etchecopar, formerly of the Society of Holy Cross. He was appointed Novice Master at 27 by St Michael. He later became the 3rd General of the Society.

this even here. M Menjoulet has approached me on the advice of his coun-
cil to admit his Community into ours. It is not difficult to realise the impli-
cations of such an undertaking, for better or worse. Pray and ask for
prayers for all this and for our houses at Orthez, Pau, Sarrance and
Mauleon.

Poor me! If God does not help me, what will happen to me this time? I
am certain that the Congregation of the Daughters of the Cross will have
the greatest share in the formation of our Society by their prayers. I hope
that if they will be good enough to redouble their prayers, God will protect
and take it forward. (Letter 92)

His fears and those of many closest to him, like Frs. Barbe, Guimon
and Chirou, did not materialise. Providence brought some very dedicated
and able priests into the Society through this amalgamation. Nine out of
the twelve members of Holy Cross joined Betharram, including the
Venerable Auguste Etchecopar, the 3rd Superior General of the Society.
From this juncture, the Bishop entrusted more and more pastoral works to
their care. Fr Garicoit's efforts amidst sufferings, and his perseverance in
spite of his fears, his application to detail amid the difficulties he faced,
and his trust and faith in God to bring about his designs; all these endeav-
ours of a generous heart would be a model for those close to him for future
pastoral works and a light to those who needed courage in the face of fear
and conflict. This proved to be the case after his death, when nearly all members voted that the vocation of the Society was to work for the Kingdom
beyond the boundaries of the Diocese of Bayonne and that it should seek this
approval from the Holy See. St Michael believed in the power of prayer...
'Pray for and ask others to pray for our little Society..... in the firm belief that
under the guidance of such a Shepherd nothing will be wanting to lead us to
safety and those many others led by us.' (Letter 92)

21. Rough Edges

Living together in community can have its own problems, especially when more and more members join. Communities can be brought to their knees when Superiors fail not only in managing human relationships, but in managing to provide for basic needs. Saints are sometimes thought to be above such trivialities; yet are these things not the raw material of charity? Fr Garicoits's letter to Sr Jerome shows he was in no way able to ignore such mundane demands. Sister had been bemoaning the fact that she had been transferred to an isolated Convent which she called a 'poor solitude' that left her with too little to do. Fr Garicoits takes up her phrase and applies it to Betharram.

Betharram. 23 Jan. 1850.

As you have now a little more time to concern yourself with Betharram, I am going to speak about this 'poor solitude'. Our poor community has 50 members, with as many priests as brothers. It seems to me that everyone is full of good intentions; but the friction of living together is very painful. It is taking so long and is so difficult, and the one who is trying to make it work at this operation has neither the necessary knowledge nor the capability; it is devastating chaos which nevertheless passes for organization in his hands. I must however confess that order is actually his abiding passion. But how can it be achieved? So you see, my dear Sister St Jerome, how we are fixed. Have you the charity to help me with your advice:

1   *How can the Brothers do the laundry properly? How can they dry the clothes and keep them clean and suitable for the poor ones that we are? In short how can they organise a good laundry?*

2   *How do we organise the kitchen?*

3   How do we organise the cellar?

4   How do we organise the Linen Room? (The linen and clothing thank God have run smoothly through the system already in operation). We have been obliged to put the Brothers in charge of the laundry this year. The Sisters at Igon had been kind enough to help us a little to start it off.

5   What can you tell us about steam cleaning?

Oh! fancy having to ask these things by letter! If only I could speak to you, but I shall have to be patient. Do tell me simply and frankly what you think might work and I shall be most grateful.

When facing difficulties, Fr Garicoits used often to say: 'God has made this work.... It is holy... It is the men employed in it who bring the obstacles. This is an undeniable fact, and God has had to intervene..... We must recognise God as the Author and Guardian of our Society; He governs it and He will protect it.' St Michael's letters cannot fail to show how he continually relied on the power of prayer, as his circular of 1862 indicates.

'Ask everyone in our Society during the 40 hours to say this prayer:

> ***O My God, do not consider my sins, but the Society which your Sacred Heart has conceived and formed. Grant it your peace, that peace which is according to your Will that alone can pacify and intimately unite all those who belong to it, with each other, with their Superiors, and with your Divine Heart; to become one, just as you are one with your Father and the Spirit. Amen. Fiat. Fiat.***

22. St Michael Garicoits and St Bernadette of Lourdes

About seven miles from Betharram, a miller's daughter, Bernadette Soubirous, in 1858 was claiming to see a lady in white at the cave of Massabielle in Lourdes. This girl claimed that the Lady asked for a chapel to be built there and that people should come and pray there for the conversion of sinners. The Lady called herself 'The Immaculate Conception'. Response from the clergy and the local authorities was not only of disbelief but also included either ridicule or hostility. The Minister of Worship, the Prefect, and Commissioner of Police held attitudes in the last category and at first terrified Bernadette with their interrogations. The families of these officials were known to the priests at Betharram. Fr Garicoits also knew the Soubirous family of the Boly Mill who had helped him with flour for his school and seminary in the stressful famine of 1846. Bernadette with her family had often come on pilgrimage to the Shrine of Our Lady of Betharram, with the great crowds numbering thousands on special feast days.

Only one curate in Lourdes, the Rev Pomian, initially paid any attention to Bernadette. The professors at the nearby seminary of St Pe were distinctly hostile. When Our Lady appeared to Bernadette in 1858, word quickly reached Betharram from lay-people who were present at the Apparitions; some believed, some did not. Fr Garicoits was spiritual director of Elfrida Lacrampe who was subsequently appointed by her Parish Priest to accompany Bernadette when she was asked to meet pilgrims. In this capacity Elfrida heard Bernadette's accounts of the Apparitions given to countless people, including many priests and Religious. Elfrida must have recounted something of these interviews to Fr Garicoits whose advice she often sought. Speaking of St Michael at his process of canonization, she recalls his influence on her life: 'I have been able to acknowledge once more his great prudence in the case of my vocation. I told him on many occasions that I wanted to enter Religious life after my 18th birthday. He always advised me not to. I now understand from the knowledge I have of myself and of the events of my life, how wise his decision was.'

Fr Garicoits knew priests, like Fr Mariotte, an Oratorian and teacher at the Seminary of St Pe who interviewed Bernadette in great detail, and Fr Dezirat, who was present when the Apparitions took place; both went to St Michael in the normal course of events for spiritual guidance. The Bishop of Lourdes had forbidden his priests to go to the Grotto. Fr Higueres of Betharram, a well-known missioner of the Society, seems to have believed Bernadette's message, since he was specifically told by Mgr Laurence to refrain from mentioning the Apparitions in his sermons. He reported to Fr Garicoits the Bishop's order. When Fr Higueres referred to the miracles which were happening, the Bishop replied: 'Even if there were miracles, there is no purpose.' St Michael remarked to Fr Higueres: 'Does Monsignor know Our Lady's purpose?'

Increasing numbers of reliable and sound-minded layfolk and priests recorded their impressions to Fr Garicoits. He was open to these experiences, but did not make public what had not been publicly approved. As pilgrims at that time were coming to Betharram in great numbers, shop-keepers there were anxious that their trade would be affected. St Michael is said to have replied that if Our Lady wanted to be honoured in Lourdes, it would not affect Betharram. His words have come true. On July 15th, 1858, Louis Veuillot, the editor of the national Catholic daily, L'Univers, was at the Spa of Bagnere near Lourdes. While there, he decided to interview Bernadette in considerable detail. In July, he stayed at Betharram. He again met Fr Garicoits in 1861 at the seminary of St Pe where he was chaplain. Louis Veuillot wrote of St Michael: 'You have a priest who, without being greatly involved in politics, could teach our great men quite a lot. He draws from the depth of his holiness safer and deeper views than those of our present day politicians.'

As crowds came in greater numbers, and even the Emperor was showing interest, Mgr Laurence could not any longer ignore the Apparitions. He turned to the Founder of the Priests of the Sacred Heart and asked him to investigate them. In July 1858, Mgr Laurence arranged for Bernadette to

be picked up and taken in his episcopal carriage to Betharram where she met Fr Garicoits.We have no account of what was said but when both were seen, they appeared full of smiles and very happy. Fr Garicoits was even more convinced of their authenticity and no doubt reported this to the Bishop. Relations between Bernadette and St Michael strengthened.

It was said that she spoke about her vocation. While the Daughters of the Cross, Sisters of Charity, Dominicans, and Carmelites were striving to attract this postulant, he directed her to the enclosed Sisters of St Bernard at Anglet. Bernadette at that time seemed drawn to this life of silence; "I will be at peace there; no one will come to annoy me any more." The Founder, Fr Cestac, who did not want extraordinary vocations, welcomed this frail confidante of Mary with warmth and affection, but refused to admit her, because of her health. St Bernadette was eventually accepted by the Sisters of Nevers.

On July 28th, which happened to be the feast of Our Lady of Betharram, Mgr Laurence set up his Commission of Enquiry, which included the Rector of the Seminary of St Pe, M Burosse and several Canons of the Diocese, who, in the course of their enquiry, took Bernadette to the Grotto and questioned her there. They were impressed by her composure, simplicity and frankness as they asked her about the details of the Apparitions.Fr Garicoit's responsibility as Superior did not allow him to visit the Grotto. A group of Daughters of the Cross with his permission went from Igon to Massabielle in September; four of them climbed through the barrier and had their names and addresses taken by the guard. The novices from Betharram went there that year and Fr Etchecopar, the novice master, went there with his parents. He noted that they spoke to the 'Mill Girl'.

During that year of the Apparitions, the numbers of pilgrims and sight-seers grew to over three thousand. With news of cures and miracles, thousands more entered the town of Lourdes. The Parish Priest, Abbe Peyremal, estimated that in 1859, Bernadette had spoken to thirty thousand enquirers, ranging from the governess of the Emperor's children, from bishops, priests and nuns to the ordinary faithful. Betharram would no doubt have heard and read about all these events.

In 1862, the Apparitions were officially recognised by Mgr Laurence.

He approved the building of a church and declared Lourdes a place of pilgrimage.

In May 1861, Bernadette wrote the first account of the Apparitions at the Grotto in a letter addressed to Fr Honore Gondrand at Betharram. He belonged to the Oblates of Mary, but since his brother had died in poverty, he obtained permission to stay at the Monastery in Betharram in order to help educate and provide for his brother's nine children. During his stay he took part in the work of the Community; he preached the Lenten Sermons at the Shrine, gave retreats to the clergy of Tarbes and missions in the area. He also came to know Bernadette and is said to have allowed her to receive Communion on Sundays. Her letter to him was no doubt in response to his request about the Apparitions.

Fr Garicoits was one of the first to raise large amounts of money for the Chapel requested by Our Lady, as this letter to Fr Barbe in Buenos Aires indicates.

The Apparition of the Immaculate Conception at the Grotto of Lourdes has just been proclaimed by Mgr Laurence, who is going to build a beautiful chapel and consecrate this new place of pilgrimage. Several of ours have been there already, notably Fr Perguilhem with our little offering. It would be perhaps well for you to send something to Mgr Laurence toward the new chapel. Write a letter to his Grace to express your joy in hearing of this new blessing for the Pyrenees. (Letter after Jan. 18th, 1862.)

At the end of January, after the announcement by Mgr Laurence, St Michael sent the offering he mentions by Fr Pierre Perguilhem; he made a further offering of five hundred francs in April, which earned him the title, Founder of the Sanctuary of Lourdes, as a letter written in June 1862 by Rev. Fourcade, secretary of the Bishop of Tarbes, records. St Michael asked all residences to support the new Sanctuary. Very soon after this letter, Fr Barbe sent a substantial offering which St Michael took in person to the Bishop in Tarbes. Mgr Laurence was so happy to welcome his former colleague, friend and generous benefactor that he gave a special dinner in his honour. He asked him to stay for the day and the following day in his own chapel, served St Michael's Mass.

As soon as St Michael was convinced that Our Lady had appeared at the grotto of Massabielle, nothing could contain his joy; 'God is good! He

Lourdes, 1872.

has filled our region with blessings.' He took a firm stand in this position even when it was hotly disputed. In spite of the general disbelief among the clergy, publications by some hostile lecturers from the Seminary in St Pe, opposition from the first Parish Priest of Lourdes and his curates, from Mgr Lacroix who forbade anyone to speak about it, and from Mgr Laurence who laughed at it, he had that wisdom which recognised the hand of God and the presence of Mary. His encouragement and repute reassured the faithful who came to consult him. One could distinguish among them certain pilgrims from the plain of Nay, some clergy and others further afield like Admiral Bruat and Louis Veuillot of **L'Univers.**

St Michael was well placed to receive news of the Apparitions from people like Rev. Estrade, author of **Apparitions de Notre Dame de Lourdes,** who knew Bernadette and her companions. She came from Lourdes to pray at the Sanctuary of Betharram on many occasions and it is said that she paid 2 sous there for the rosary which she used during the Apparitions. After the Apparitions ended, she returned to Betharram with her mother, in thanksgiving. Many years later, her nephew studied at the College and entered the Society at Betharram. He worked and died as a priest among the poor in Buenos Aires.

Although there was only a year and four months to his death, one finds St Michael on at least three occasions among the crowds kneeling before the Grotto; on one occasion with the director of the Seminary of Bayonne, Canon Poure. He recalled at the process for St Michael's canonization:

'Fr Garicoits witnessed the growth of the pilgrimages to Lourdes not only without distress, but with marked joy; something which I noticed myself when I went on pilgrimage there with him in those early years.'(Canon Poure. Letter 398).

23. Wider Fields

In 1851, the Bishop requested St Michael to take on the Parish and church of St Louis Gonzaga which was built by the Jesuits in Pau well before the Revolution. As it had been repossessed in 1851, the town made a request to the Bishop for a priest. He turned to Betharram. Fr Garicoits sent Fr Vignau, one of his first companions. As it was in a rather insalubrious neighbourhood, the change that this apostolic priest gradually effected was noted by Mgr Lacroix's successor. 'This quarter,' he said, 'not being known then for its excellent reputation, was raised, cleaned up and is what we see it to be today; all by Fr Vignau's presence; a community of good, devout, and industrious people.' They came to the services at church and listened to his simple and good-natured homilies. He was chaplain to the boarding-school beside the church, and to the sewing class for girls run by the Daughters of the Cross as well as being chaplain to them and to the Ursulines.

The Sanctuary of Our Lady at Sarrance, which records mention as far back as 1343, was confided to the Society by Bishop Lacroix. In 1835, the parish priest, Fr Larrieu, requested to enter the Society and proposed that the Society should look after the shrine. At that time, the shrine, having been confiscated in the Revolution, was only legally re-acquired in 1851. St Michael sent one of his first companions, Fr Larrouy, to refound this centre of ancient pilgrimages. Restoration began on the Church in 1856 and the present Way of the Cross was constructed two years later. All this took place through the influence of St Michael. Great devotions recommenced in honour of Our Lady. St Michael himself came to the sanctuary to say Mass and invest fifty Children of Mary with their medals, on one occasion.

At times, the pressure of all responsibility became overwhelming and as for anyone, there is the temptation, as he once said: 'The thought of my responsibility at God's Judgement Seat frightened me and at times I was tempted to run away. Ibarre, my native village, came into my dreams. My dear old Father..How pleasant to spend the remaining years of my life there! The Mass Offerings would be enough to keep me; and anyhow, if need be, I could still do a bit of digging. If only I could see again my dear old church, so poor and yet so pretty! In my imagination I can see it there on the hill, the little river, Bidouze flowing nearby. I would go begging to decorate it, if necessary. Thoughts like these have come into my mind, but I realise that they are temptations.'

God is the Author of our undertaking, therefore if it is holy, He will protect it. Hope is an immovable rock on which to build and to withstand all temptations. There is never more reason to hope than when all seems hopeless.

Church at Sarrance today.

104

24. Mission to South America

A mid the harsh conditions of life in the Basque country in the 1850s, the lure of a better life in Argentina promoted by the new government began to attract increasing numbers of Basque families, at first from Spain, where civil war had decimated the land. Although priests thundered from their pulpits against the loss of the faith by going to this foreign land, the flow of immigrants continued. The Argentine Consul asked for chaplains to accompany them. It is said that Fr Guimon also approached Mgr Lacroix to send Basque priests to minister to the ever increasing numbers. The Bishop approached the Missioners of Hasparren, but they declined. In 1854, he turned to Betharram, to Fr Garicoits's surprise, especially as the Society was fully stretched in founding schools. Fr Garicoits called a general meeting. The outcome was that twenty out of twenty-one members agreed that they should accept the Bishop's request. Practically everyone was willing to go. It was decided that two of the first members should go: Frs Guimon and Larrouy, with Fr Didace Barbe, the Assistant to St Michael and headmaster of the College of Betharram. With them were two other Basque priests, Frs Harbustan and Sardoy, and a student, Jean Magendie, and two Brothers, Joannes and Fabien.

After a long and dangerous voyage lasting two months, they reached Buenos Aires in November, 1856. Soon after they arrived, they began preaching and catechising the young. Fr Garicoits intended founding a College as well as the Mission Apostolate. In 1858, the future College of St Jose was founded by Fr Barbe, assisted by the student, Jean Magendie, and Br Joannes. The other members set up another community whose purpose was to give missions in Buenos Aires and beyond. In 1861, Fr Harbustan was sent to Montevideo in Uruguay to minister to the French and Basque emigrees. After various vicissitudes, he built the Church of the Immaculate Conception.

St. Michael kept in regular correspondence with everyone. Jean Magendie wrote asking for his blessing. Almost like a patriarch, he replies: *Yes, yes, with all my heart. I send you the blessing of an old man and a Father and wish that it stays with you all your life and till your dying breath... Pray for us and for your brother* (whom he hoped would join the Society but he did not.) *Be always Homo idoneus, expeditus et expositus. (Capable, always available and detached). This is the infallible way of being the crown and joy of your Superiors, of the Church and of God Himself. (Letter 140).* Writing to Br Joannes who had been a pioneer in so many foundations: *I am delighted to know that you are happy in your post with those in your Community, especially Fr. Barbe. This convinces me that you are no longer listening to your negative self.*

Continue my dear Friend to look positively upwards with no other rule of behaviour, no other motive for consolation than doing the good pleasure of God. God wills it (Dieu le veut...which was the battle cry of Joan of Arc).... *Your two sisters in the Convent are well... The third is thinking of entering.*

My dear Brother. See how much you owe to your vocation, and for all the blessings you and your Sisters have received in their vocation. Thank God for it.

A thousand greetings from your sisters, your father and mother..Pray for us who pray for you.. (Letter 141)

Fr Barbe had little support and at first opposition from the Community when founding the College. Pupil numbers vacillated between four and twenty and funds were scarce. Fr Garicoits had to write to Fr Larrouy.

What has been done, has been done with the knowledge of the Bishops of Buenos Aires and Bayonne and of the Superior at Betharram. The objective of the work is this: you have been loaned to the Bishop of Buenos Aires for the mission to the Basques and Bearnais,but the work of a College is not opposed to the work of preaching Missions.

It is in order to write to me about your doubts, but to go beyond that, is to go against the Rule.. (Letter157)

The foundation of the College went ahead.

St Michael believed in the power of common prayer and for that reason supported the Apostleship of Prayer in this letter to Fr Barbe. *If you can make arrangements with the post office I am going to send you an Apostolate of Prayer booklet which I recommend for your use. It will be a source of many graces and a most powerful means of saving souls, as you will see. I will send you the leaflets of enrolment when I have the list of names of those who wish to join. This association will not interfere with other associations but will augment them..*

Pray for the Church, especially for the Pope and for our members. Be apostles of prayer in Corde Christi.

Even from this distance, he wrote to them in a way that expressed his deep feelings for each.

You can tell Fr Harbustan, as you can tell everyone else how much I always love them and how much I like to place them very often before Our Lord as children of His Heart, saying 'O Lord, no one is a Father like Yourself; here are Your children, children of Your Heart.'(Letter 342)

When considering whether to take on a new work, he did not lose sight of his vision for the Society.

In regard to the Chaplaincy of St Jean, you know what I think. We should lend ourselves as valued helpers, never as embarrassments, nor obstacles; not invoking our Constitutions, real or imaginary, as we reply to the Bishop, nor causing difficulty as helpers. Let us realise what we are and what our spirit is all about..... never being unsure of our strength, but putting into practice the great commandment of brotherly love, being more ready to look on the good side rather than being negative and judgmental. Try to justify the intention even when it is not possible to justify the action. If it is not possible to justify the intention, exercise charity by not neglecting one's duty or by failing in good manners. (Letter 377)

From these letters we learn how sensitive he was to people's hardships and how he did not fail to praise courage. When he heard of the situation faced by Fr Harbustan in Montevideo and the Vicar Apostolic Monsignor Vera, who was expelled from his church by the government, he expressed his support for Fr Barbe's offer of hospitality and Fr Harbustan's courage.

We read with much concern about the sufferings of Mgr Vera. On this occasion, you have rightly understood my sentiments, as you always do. I support whatever you do for this worthy minister of Jesus Christ. Yes, because of his exile.. we should be happy and honoured to welcome him among you. I have wept tears of joy while reading of your offer of shelter to this much loved and persecuted man. I would have done the same myself. (Letter 380)

Shortly after this, Fr Harbustan had a warrant issued for his arrest for refusing to accept the priest appointed by the Government and upholding the displaced Mgr Vera, who had been appointed by the Holy See. He managed to evade the police and fled to the French Consulate from where he was put on board a French warship set for Buenos Aires.

'There you are, a confessor of the Faith!' Fr Garicoits writes. *'We hope that God will turn what you have experienced to His greater glory and our good. We will not fail to pray for you to Our Lady.' (Letter 619)*

There was a conflict over their missionary boundaries which arose from Fr Guimon's desire to be independent of the restrictions of Mgr Lacroix and to take his mission to the Indians. He was supported by other Bishops but not from Bayonne or Buenos Aires. The Society was considering applying with the support of higher authority for the status of Apostolic Missionaries which would put them directly under the Holy See. St Michael may have feared a split in the Society through this action. He wrote to Fr Barbe: *I am entirely opposed to the idea of the Apostolic Missionary. What will it achieve? It is only a stratagem to by-pass the Bishops over here and over there.*

I see no reason to change.... But when people have fixed ideas it is difficult to argue. They believe they are losing time when they cannot have things their way. They do not know how to appreciate and embrace corde magno et animo volenti et constanti (with a generous heart and constant will) *the obscurity, the sterility and lack of success to which they see themselves reduced by obedience. This is unfortunately the manna which still remains hidden from very many.*

What can you do? It is necessary to take people as they are and draw from them the best while knowing how to suffer. For the rest we must accept limits. Let us support each other and certainly the good God will support us. (Letter 490)

His New Year's greeting to the Community of San Jose in January, 1863, which elaborates on the Constitution of the Society of Jesus, adopted by his Society, illustrates his constant attention to the spiritual growth of individual members as well as the spiritual growth of the Community. This would be his last letter for New Year:

A happy New Year to all of you across the sea and, a year full of spiritual riches.... in the school of Our Lord.

He often distilled the fruit of his meditations in these letters, as he does here. These reflections from the readings of Christmas go right to the heart of his life which is drawn from his vision of the Incarnation: the mystery that God with all His power and truth and love could become man. *Be true worshippers and devout observers of this mystery and teaching, not accepting anything that would not be true to His human behaviour or unworthy of His holiness, nothing untrue in His freedom... Drive away the dark clouds of worldly ways in your behaviour, and seek to be enlightened with the eyes of faith and shielded from the confusing haze of worldly wisdom. (Pope Leo the Great)*

In this way you will not entertain unseemly behaviour and desires, and all members of the Society will live balanced, just, and holy lives (Letter 390)

25. Forward to the End

In 1853, Fr Garicoits had a stroke; he had to leave Betharram and convalesce at the Chateau de Balliencourt in Valencienne in Northern France. He attributed his recovery to prayer. *'After God, it was the prayers said for me at Betharram and at Igon that brought about my recovery.'*(94) The enormous amount of concern and expressions of affection manifested on this occasion touched him deeply. *'I am embarrassed,'* he writes to a Daughter of the Cross in 1853 *'to receive so many heartfelt good wishes.... So for once can I not say Deo Gratias! Yes, Thank God a thousand times for the attention that your holy congregation has shown me! I have such confidence in those prayers and Holy Communions that have given you such sentiments for me, so that the very thought of this has driven away all my fears. They pray, they will continue to pray for me, they will gain for me all the graces that I need so much. If you only knew all the good that this thought on so many occasions has done for me. You will continue, will you not, to give me this help which is more and more necessary?' (Letter 100)*

Some days of rest sufficed to put him back on his feet and apparently leave no trace of the stroke. He wrote on January 24th 1854: *'I believe that I am now better than I was before I became ill. Pray that I will be able to use all my energy for the good of souls and the greater glory of God.' (Letter 100)*

The following year he had another relapse; while apparently less violent than the first, this made those close to him uneasy. He used to say to them, 'Don't be upset. We will last as long as the Lord wants.'

After that, he suffered a series of relapses. More than once, he believed the end had come, yet he always seemed to recover. At the beginning of 1863, he was struck down with violent fits of coughing and paralysing stomach cramps. During Lent, there was cause for alarm. He had to stay in bed for three weeks. With the warm weather of April his pain passed. He believed he had recovered and wished to make use of this apparent recovery to visit the Bishop. It was Easter Week. When he arrived, his friends in Bayonne saw in him a great change. As he left them, they feared that they would never see him again. One lady did not conceal her distress in seeing him so thin and weak. 'Fr Garicoits,' she said quite bluntly, 'you will not be with us for long.' With a smile, he replied, 'May God's will be done. We will meet in Heaven.'

For some time, the thought of his approaching journey to Heaven became part of his conversation, yet it was expressed without any drama, but quite simply and as a matter of fact.

When he made a long desired visit to the Anghelus at Oneix where he had worked as a farm hand and from where he had made his First Communion that set him on his journey for God, he said at the tearful moment of leaving: 'We will no longer see each other in this world but only in Heaven.'

During his weekly conference in July of 1862, after he had given some advice and pointed out certain practical actions concerning various problems, he added: 'I am asking nothing for myself, I am sixty-five and about to go to the next world. But it is in the name of God that I ask you, as one who is ready to stand before Him.' During Lent of 1863, Fr Higueres, before going to give a mission, went to his room to take his leave and go to Confession. Fr Garicoits said to him: 'I am going to resign as Superior; I feel I am about to die.' After this, he suffered a series of relapses. Towards the end of April, while he was at Igon, he collapsed and became so ill that they thought he was going to die. One of the priests and the sisters came to his assistance. He said as he saw them, 'Carry on, let us go to Heaven.'

He recovered while convalescing at Igon, but scarcely had this happened when he was thinking of taking up his work and returning to Betharram to give the Missioners a retreat with the Spiritual Exercises. The doctor had to intervene to stop him. He gave this task to Fr Etchecopar, to whom he said, 'I do not know what will happen. Whatever it is, it will be what God wishes.'

The fears of his friends and his own estimations were only too well-founded. He had taken some days of relaxation at Betharram when he suffered another relapse. It was the Saturday before the Ascension, towards ten o'clock in the evening. Unlike his usual habit of not wanting to disturb anyone, he called for the Infirmarian, who slept beside his room. He was pale, sweating profusely and finding it very difficult to breathe. The brother felt his pulse, which was racing. He changed his linen and bed-clothes and gave him some warm water, which made him sick. The pain eased and Fr Garicoïts persuaded the Brother to go back to bed, which he did. It was midnight. The Brother woke early that morning and went see how he was. To his utter amazement, the room was empty. He went down to the sacristy and found him vested and ready to go onto the altar!

On Sunday and Monday, he was not too bad. On Tuesday, in the afternoon, he believed he was well enough to go and see the Bishop, who was making a pastoral visit in the area. The Sister Superior managed to persuade him not to go because the journey would be too far and painful for him that day, but the following day, the Bishop would be nearer to Betharram. He accepted this advice. As the sisters had heard of his arrival at the convent, they all gathered in the gallery which looked down on the parlour. They asked him to bless all the Community; something which he had always refused to do. They were very happy to see that he agreed. He blessed them and said, 'Always go forward till you reach Heaven.' ('En avant toujours, jusqu'au ciel.') It proved to be the final blessing of a Father to his children in God.

He returned to Betharram. The following day, he got ready to travel to Nay where he called on the Dominican Sisters and the Curate, then he set off to Mirepeix where the Bishop was staying. 'I received him on his arrival,' said the Parish priest of Nay in his deposition later.

'I have come to say goodbye,' he said to me.

'Not yet,' I replied.

'Yes, yes,' he replied, 'I feel very ill.'

We entered the Bishop's room. He prostrated himself at his feet and said: 'Monsignor, give me your last blessing.'

'You're not there yet,' he replied. 'I hope we can still keep you.'

I have never forgotten the impression that this scene made on me. The deep spirit of faith with which he prostrated himself before the Bishop as though it was before the Lord Himself as he asked for his blessing. I must add that the face of Michael Garicoits, although deathly pale, conveyed an expression of perfect peace and inner joy. The sisters whom he had visited the previous day told me that they felt the same.

Monsignor was visibly moved and as though held back by respect seemed to hesitate in blessing this humble old man kneeling at his feet. Then he gave it on condition that he promised to take more care of his health, having aggravated its condition, and henceforth to do less work. Like a child he promised, while excusing himself for as yet having done nothing for the glory of God. The Bishop blessed him and embraced him with tears in his eyes.

On his return, he stopped at the convent in Igon. The effort of all this had drained him. Fr Higueres found him there. He and the curate were preparing the children for Confirmation. Shocked by the ghastly pallor of his complexion, he told the Brother who was his driver to take him immediately to Betharram. Fr Garicoits saw the shocked look in Fr Higuere's face and said with a smile, 'Do you want to keep a corpse alive? It isn't worth it.' Then he said to the curate, 'I was pleased to see the Bishop. All is set in place for the best. May the will of God be done.'

He returned to Betharram before supper, saw the Brother in the kitchen and asked for some soup. He wanted him to take a substantial meal but he said, 'Soup is enough.' The brother forcefully insisted, to which he replied, 'As you wish. Let us go ahead always. We must accept what the good God sends us.' To which the Brother replied, 'Yes, and sometimes by force.' Fr Garicoits replied, 'By force? Oh no! It is not necessary to receive what the good God sends us by force, but with respect and love.'

Up to the very end he looked into tiny details of life with all members of the Community. He showed without great display and effortlessly the perfect union of his soul with God.

After supper with the Community, he went into the Common Room for recreation and was cheerful. He gave instructions about the Bishop's reception on the feast of the Ascension for the children's Confirmation the next day and that he was to be received as Our Lord Himself. He wished everyone a happy and holy feast. Little did the Community realise that this was his final farewell.

Having said his prayers, he went to bed and to sleep. At two o'clock, a serious fit of coughing awoke him with a start. This had become frequent but that night, it continued with increasing violence. 'I heard him call,' said the Brother Infirmarian, 'and I got up. He was having grave difficulty in breathing. I tried the usual methods which had succeeded before; it was useless. As he got worse, I called others.' Fr Bursar arrived first and found him in a state of extreme pain; he was scarcely breathing, but choking. Then Fr Fondeville, his confessor arrived, followed by Fr Saubatte. They spoke of sending for the doctor, but he would not hear of it. 'It is not worth the trouble.' Being, as he knew, in mortal danger he asked for the Sacrament of Reconciliation and received absolution. Frs Cazaban and Saubatte knelt beside the bed and said the prayers for the dying. He asked if they could open the window to help him breathe, to which they replied it was too cold. He insisted. Immediately, his pain seemed to ease. He raised his eyes and cried, 'It is finished. My God, come to my help.' Fr Fondeville began the prayers for the Anointing of the Sick, or as they were called then, of Extreme Unction. While he was being anointed, Fr Garicoits lay back his head as if to sleep and murmured these final words: 'Miserere mei, Deus, secundum magnam misericordiam tuam,' (Have mercy on me, O God, according to Your great mercy.) and breathed his last. It was Thursday, 14 May, 1863, the Feast of the Ascension, at three o'clock in the morning, the hour he sometimes rose to begin his prayer and work.

News spread rapidly. At 7 am, the Bishop had arrived to share the Community's grief.

His body was laid out in priestly vestments in the Sanctuary of Our Lady, until Saturday. Great numbers of people came from Pau, Tarbes, Bayonne and the surrounding area, to see the body of this saintly priest for the last time. People filed past from morning to evening; some touching his mortal remains with medals, rosaries, books, cloth, vestments. Public veneration swelled to people wanting relics so that it was necessary to guard his remains. Two priests had to direct the crowds. Some kissed his hands or his feet. Mothers brought their infants, and the poor, as if they understood he was their friend, filed past. Mgr Lacroix arrived on Friday evening. He entered the chapel with tears in his eyes and knelt before the body and murmured: 'There he is then, this saint and incomparable friend that the Lord has just called to heaven!' He touched the body with his pectoral cross, his breviary and his rosary.

Here we have one man of vision and wisdom who said, 'I am nothing,' yet he helped spread that fire which the Lord in His love had cast on earth. In God's Providence, he was part of the religious revival growing throughout the Catholic world in the 19th century, in which over six hundred new religious communities were founded. In France, between 1800 and 1880, two hundred thousand women entered Religious communities, and by 1880, thirty thousand men and one hundred and thirty thousand women were in the Religious life in France. The Spirit of God fanned such souls of fire into a force that achieved wonders in bringing Christian values and hope among the 19th century poor of Europe, and a force whose fruits have brought education and dignity to many Third World nations today. St Michael Garicoïts was an apostle of God's love in the renewal of Christian education, and of the values in family life through schools and missions. Guided by such men and women who were attentive to the Spirit of God, thousands of young aspirants joined the call to Religious life, taking up the challenge of prayer and service.

Many came to seek St Michael's counsel: bishops, priests, people in public and professional life, and ordinary folk of all ages. Many were indebted to him for guidance in a choice of life and in the resolution of moral problems. Some came for retreats under his guidance. His correspondence was enormous. He would enlighten, uplift, purify and sanctify.

This is how one of his contemporaries remembered him. 'I fancy I can see his venerable face, his serene forehead radiating a kindness which shows through its apparent severity. His bushy eyebrows jutting out over his eyes alight with sympathy and gentleness; that smile on his lips, so kind and affectionate as to captivate all who had the pleasure of speaking with him. And yet his conversation was straightforward, unstudied, gentle, rambling along apparently unaware of itself; but in reality it was bursting with the creative energy of the Word of God. It begot everything out of nothing; good-will, works and institutions.' (Canon Poiré)

Fr Estrate of the Society recalls: 'I can still see his kind and peaceful look; his head slightly inclined as if to give the kiss of peace; his sure step, brisk at times; that unfailing smile of welcome as he listened patiently; the supernatural words which always came from his lips; his thoughtfulness for others and his irresistible desire to please. I can still hear his hearty laugh with its ring unaffected and sincere; the grave and moving tone of his prayers as he knelt motionless in adoration before the tabernacle.'

His life had been inspired by all those holy men and women in his early formative years, when the Spirit's Power took hold of the Church of his day. He was an expression of the Sacred Heart's all-consuming love. Faithful to this inspiration, his life was an expression of the Incarnate Word of God Who said to His heavenly Father from the outset of His entrance into the world: 'Here I am. I come to do your will.' St Michael's life shows the power of love, and how it is the key to any lasting human achievement. In this school of love, he had learnt to respond instantly, irrevocably, and unreservedly, to the end.

The Heart of Jesus burning with love had inflamed his heart to cast fire on earth; a fire that will not be quenched.

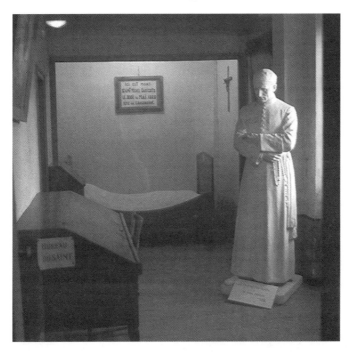

St Michael's room.

116

Appendix

St Michael's Method for discerning the will of God

In the changing patterns of today's world, many people are asking questions about Life and seeking answers as to where this change is leading; questions ranging from the reason for Life itself, and for what is its purpose. Others wonder where God is in all this. Those who believe may ask what does God want me to be, or what does He want me to do? The Church is sent by Christ to teach all nations and has inherited His teaching. Throughout its existence, it has developed a tradition of guidance based on God's word which has been applied by saintly and wise men and women inspired by God's Spirit to speak to their generation, and pass on this inheritance to the present world. Among these is St Michael Garicoits(1797-1863). He guided many in his time with what he called a method for discerning the will of God.

His method comes from the Gospels and the Church's long tradition in spiritual direction and his own long experience, not just in dealing with others but in dealing with his own behaviour and inner attitudes. 'Do not precede the Spirit but follow.' All these ways were lived by himself as he tried to discover the Will of God, beginning with his vocation to be a founder to the minutest details of his daily life. His conduct was modelled on the love expressed by Jesus for His heavenly Father. To discover where God is, he started from where a person was, and required fidelity there. Here is a summary of his method.

1. **Be faithful to the present situation**, which means doing what God expects in one's present position and occupation. This principle is based on the Lord's words; 'He who is faithful in that which is little, will be faithful in that which is great.' The uncertainties of life today and the erosion of Christian principles have caused a certain amount of unreliability, rootlessness and permissiveness. Many need to be

brought back to a firm foundation for their lives so that they are able to see God's will. St Michael like St Paul believed that to discern God's will requires perseverance and faithfulness which 'wins the crown of eternal life.'

2. **Certain dispositions** prevent one's recognising the will of God. St Michael following St Ignatius of Loyola calls these dispositions; 'disordered desires.' It is not always easy to become aware of such obstacles, which may be the result of influences from the home or from significant role models in one's early upbringing. St Michael, through his perception and wisdom, helped many to become aware of such disordered desires in their lives and challenged them to change. Sometimes, he offered them practical as well as spiritual ways and means for action.

    'If you see a beam in your brother's eye, take out the log in your own first.' **Get rid of disordered desires.** 'Blessed are the clean of heart, they shall see God.'

3. **Conform your life to Christ's.** In times of difficulty, he continually encouraged those in positions of responsibility not to be afraid to carry the Cross with perseverance and courage. It is no less important today as yesterday to do what is right and just, in spite of the pain it might inflict upon us. Jesus exhorted His followers in the Sermon on the Mount. 'Blessed are the peacemakers.... those who suffer in the cause of righteousness...' St Michael's letters convey this message in terms which are relevant today. Many carry the Cross without following Christ, but St Michael maintained that those who carry their Cross with Christ will gain lasting redemption and everlasting life.

    St Michael's message was that all who are striving courageously for peace and justice or for whatever is right in these present times can find God's will through following Christ's example....

4. **Open your life to the saving will of God.** Many people are quite content to be left alone; undisturbed in their lives. Change is hard enough when it is thrust upon us and most would prefer to do without it. To be open to God means being ready to change and be changed. St Michael uses a word which has gone out of fashion but is as real today as it ever was: the word 'abandon.' To abandon

oneself to God's will means among other things to give up personal possessions, power, security and to rely on Him for the call He makes. All are called to do this at times and to varying degrees in life. Not to be open to change is not to be open to God.

5. **Pray.** Be directed by the Holy Spirit. He applied St Paul's teaching that 'No one can say 'Jesus is Lord' unless he is under the influence of the Holy Spirit.' Rom.12;3. St Michael always said: 'Do not precede but follow the Holy Spirit.'

The Spirit leads us to pray and to all truth. 'The Spirit comes to help us in our weakness... in a way we could never put into words.... and God who knows perfectly what is in our hearts, knows perfectly well what He means... The pleas of the faithful expressed by the Spirit are according to the mind of God.' Rom.8;26-27.

God's will is not found in someone else's direction but comes from within. When helping others St Michael believed it was important to find what is going on within: in their heart; in their feelings.

6. **Self-examination** for the signs of God's will. This method is based on the nature of God who is essentially good, but it is not easy to apply or recognise and in some cases requires a spiritual counsellor of considerable experience and wisdom. St Ignatius spoke of discovering the signs of God's will from our feelings in regard to a particular decision or course of action: feelings of consolation which come from God and desolation which come from the devil. In simple terms what comes from God brings peace; this is consolation; and what comes from the 'enemy' brings worry and a feeling of unease sooner or later; this is desolation. Many books have been and will continue to be written on this principle which St Michael applied in his letters and when he gave counsel.

7. **He was very practical.** To reach a conclusion God expects us to use our intelligence. This means adding up the pros and cons either of a situation or in deciding a course of action.... Jesus spoke of a general deliberating whether he should take his army to battle, but first he sits down and counts the odds for and against him. In the same way God's will is ascertained by **analysing what is for or against our decision.**

8.   **What pleases God** ultimately brings not division but unity; it creates community and communion. This was another sign to look for in finding God's will.

9.   **The need for a spiritual helper.** It is not possible to always see ourselves as others see us or as God sees us; there is a need for an outsider with faith who is capable of listening not only to what we say but of perceiving what lies behind our words; our hopes, our fears, our joys, our sorrows, and recognises the negative voices and the positive voices in what we say. St Michael spoke of competent directors. Today it is questioned whether directors who give directions are needed, but there is no doubt that all can profit from spiritual helpers, or as some call them soul friends, or co-journeyers or spiritual counsellors. Through these men and women one can discover God's will. St Michael made no distinction between directors and supervisors, but today the latter are becoming recognised as necessary as in the secular world for those who are engaged in spiritual counselling.

10. **Challenge to action.** After one had completed these steps and consulted one's spiritual helper and found where God's will lay. St Michael challenged the person from that moment to respond to God with generosity, courage, and faithfulness; to act 'without delay, without looking back and without any reservations'. St Michael always looked into the heart. If he found a predominance of love, he gave great encouragement. This method relies entirely on love from start to finish. So the challenge is to show love and the reason for taking action is from love rather than any other motive.

11. **In as much as one responds** in this manner, one will always be at peace and experience true joy.

Life of St Michael

Bibliography

La Vie et l'Oeuvre du Vénérable Michel Garicoits	B Bourdenne scj
Correspondance de Saint Michel Garicoits Vol 1, 2. 3	Pierre Miéyaa scj
Pensées de St Michel Garicoits	A Etchécopar scj
Doctrine Spirituelle de St Michel Garicoits	P Duvignau scj
La Maitre de la Vie Spirituelle	P Duvignau sci
Articles presented at Betharram in 1985	
Histoire de l'Eglise de France au temps de St Michel	Abbe Laulom
Temps d'étude de Michel Garicoits	V. Landel scj
Michel Garicoits à Cambo	G Verley scj
Au Grande Séminaire de Bétharram	M Gandolfi scj
Pensée philosophique et affaire de Lammenais	A Mansanné scj
Theological Formation	M Zappa scj
Le Père Garicoits et Soeur Elizabeth Bichier des Ages	Sr Marie de Magdala
Le Père Garicoits et Père Leblanc	V Landel scj
Le Père Garicoits et la Première Communauté	G Spini scj
Missions diocesaines au temps de St Michel	A Mansanné scj
L'enseignement au temps de Michel Garicoits	P Carricart scj
Le Père Garicoits et les Religieux Frères	G Verley scj
Michael Garicoits	A Brunot scj
A Short Life of St Michael Garicoits	P Collier scj
Bernadette vous parle	R Laurentin
Les écrits de St Bernadette et sa voie spirituelle	A Ravier sj
Notre Dame de Bétharram	R Descomps scj
Le Voyant de Bétharram et la Voyante de Lourdes	Oyhenart scj
Outline History of the Catholic Church	R Walker
History of Europe	A Alison
The Peninsula Veterans	D S Richards
The Peninsula War (1807-1814)	M. Glover
La Bataille d'Orthez (Revue de Pau et du Bearn N 15)	P M Stephen
Histoire de la vie de St Michel Garicoits	P Mieyaa scj
The Rise and Fall of Catholic Religious Orders	P Wittburg